First World War
and Army of Occupation
War Diary
France, Belgium and Germany

15 DIVISION
46 Infantry Brigade
Royal Scots (Lothian Regiment)
9th Battalion
1 February 1918 - 31 May 1919

WO95/1954/1

The Naval & Military Press Ltd
www.nmarchive.com
Published in association with The National Archives

Published by

The Naval & Military Press Ltd

Unit 10 Ridgewood Industrial Park,

Uckfield, East Sussex,

TN22 5QE England

Tel: +44 (0) 1825 749494

www.naval-military-press.com

www.nmarchive.com

This diary has been reprinted in facsimile from the original. Any imperfections are inevitably reproduced and the quality may fall short of modern type and cartographic standards.

© **Crown Copyright**
Images reproduced by permission of The National Archives, London, England, 2015.

Contents

Document type	Place/Title	Date From	Date To
Heading	WO95/1954/1		
Heading	15th Division 46th Brigade 9th Bn Royal Scots Regt Feb 1918-May 1919 From 51 Div 154 Bde		
Heading	61st Division 183rd Infy Bde 9th Bn Royal Scots Feb-May 1918		
Heading	Vol 36 War Diary 9th Battn (Hrs) The Royal Scots. 1st February 1918 To 28th February 1918 Vol 36		
Miscellaneous	Cover for Documents. Nature of Enclosures.		
War Diary	Bailleulval	01/02/1918	01/02/1918
War Diary	Bailleulval Courcelles Le Comte	02/02/1918	02/02/1918
War Diary	Courcelles	03/02/1918	06/02/1918
War Diary	Curchy	07/02/1918	09/02/1918
War Diary	Germaine	10/02/1918	11/02/1918
War Diary	Line	12/02/1918	22/02/1918
War Diary	Beauvois	23/02/1918	28/02/1918
Operation(al) Order(s)	Operation Order No. 145	01/02/1918	01/02/1918
Operation(al) Order(s)	Operation Order No. 146	05/02/1918	05/02/1918
Operation(al) Order(s)	Operation Order No. 147	08/02/1918	08/02/1918
Operation(al) Order(s)	Operation Order No. 148	10/02/1918	10/02/1918
Operation(al) Order(s)	Addendum To Operation Order No. 148	11/02/1918	11/02/1918
Operation(al) Order(s)	Operation Order No. 149	14/02/1918	14/02/1918
Operation(al) Order(s)	Operation Order No 150	18/02/1918	18/02/1918
Operation(al) Order(s)	Operation Order No 151	19/02/1918	19/02/1918
Operation(al) Order(s)	Distribution		
Operation(al) Order(s)	Operation Order No. 152	21/02/1918	21/02/1918
War Diary	Beauvois	01/03/1918	02/03/1918
War Diary	Line	03/03/1918	10/03/1918
War Diary	Marteville	11/03/1918	19/03/1918
War Diary	Beauvois	20/03/1918	21/03/1918
War Diary	Line	22/03/1918	25/03/1918
War Diary	Le Quesnel	26/03/1918	26/03/1918
War Diary	Line	27/03/1918	30/03/1918
War Diary	Gentelles	31/03/1918	31/03/1918
Heading	183rd Brigade. 61st Division. 1/9th Battalion The Royal Scots Regiment April 1918		
War Diary	Gentelles.	01/04/1918	01/04/1918
War Diary	Line.	02/04/1918	02/04/1918
War Diary	Briquemesnil.	03/04/1918	03/04/1918
War Diary	Vergies	04/04/1918	10/04/1918
War Diary	Steenbecque.	11/04/1918	11/04/1918
War Diary	Line	12/04/1918	12/04/1918
War Diary	St. Venant.	13/04/1918	13/04/1918
War Diary	Line	14/04/1918	24/04/1918
War Diary	St. Venant.	25/04/1918	26/04/1918
War Diary	Line.	27/04/1918	30/04/1918
War Diary	Drafts. Estimated Casualties.		
Heading	War Diary 9th Bn. (Hrs) The Royal Scots 1st May 1918-31st May, 1918 Vol 38		
War Diary	Asile D'Ailennes St Venant	01/05/1918	03/05/1918
War Diary	Line	04/05/1918	08/05/1918

War Diary	Asile D'Ailennes St Venant.		09/05/1918	12/05/1918
War Diary	Line		13/05/1918	16/05/1918
War Diary	Asile D'Ailennes St Venant		17/05/1918	20/05/1918
War Diary	Line		21/05/1918	24/05/1918
War Diary	Asile D'Ailennes St Venant		25/05/1918	31/05/1918
War Diary	9 Roy Scots Vol 39 War Diary came from 61 Div 1.6.18 June 18 May 19			
War Diary	Molinghem		01/06/1918	01/06/1918
War Diary	Arras		02/06/1918	06/06/1918
War Diary	Wakefield Camp.		07/06/1918	09/06/1918
War Diary	Line.		10/06/1918	25/06/1918
War Diary	Wakefield Camp		26/06/1918	30/06/1918
War Diary	Confidential Vol 40 War Diary 9th Battn Hrs. The Royal Scots. July 1918. Vol 40			
Miscellaneous	Cover for Documents. Nature of Enclosures.			
War Diary	Wakefield Camp. Near Arras		01/07/1918	03/07/1918
War Diary	Line		04/07/1918	12/07/1918
War Diary	Arras		13/07/1918	13/07/1918
War Diary	Cambligneul		14/07/1918	16/07/1918
War Diary	Ref Map Beauvais Spec Sheet No 32 Moncaux		17/07/1918	19/07/1918
War Diary	Haute Fontaine		20/07/1918	21/07/1918
War Diary	Foret Dominale De Retz		22/07/1918	22/07/1918
War Diary	Line		23/07/1918	25/07/1918
War Diary	Line & Chaudun		26/07/1918	28/07/1918
War Diary	Line		29/07/1918	31/07/1918
Operation(al) Order(s)	Operation Order No. 14 Ref Map 51B N.W. 1/20,000		02/07/1918	02/07/1918
Operation(al) Order(s)	Operation Order No. 15 Ref Map 51B-N.W. 1/20,000		08/07/1918	08/07/1918
Operation(al) Order(s)	Operation Order No. 16 Ref Map 51A 1/20,000		11/07/1918	11/07/1918
Operation(al) Order(s)	Administrative Instruction issued with Operation Order No 16		11/07/1918	11/07/1918
Operation(al) Order(s)	Operation Order No 17 Ref Map 51C-NE 1/20000		12/07/1918	12/07/1918
Operation(al) Order(s)	Operation Order No 17A		15/07/1918	15/07/1918
Operation(al) Order(s)	Operation Order No 18		22/07/1918	22/07/1918
Operation(al) Order(s)	Administrative Instructions No 2		11/07/1918	11/07/1918
Heading	War Diary 9th Battn (Hrs) The Royal Scots From 1.8.18 to 31.8.18 Vol 41			
War Diary	Line		01/08/1918	03/08/1918
War Diary	Souchy Monceaux		04/08/1918	04/08/1918
War Diary	Monceaux		05/08/1918	06/08/1918
War Diary	Maizieres		07/08/1918	17/08/1918
War Diary	Arras		18/08/1918	24/08/1918
War Diary	Marqueffles Huts		25/08/1918	25/08/1918
War Diary	Mazincarbe		26/08/1918	27/08/1918
War Diary	Line		28/08/1918	31/08/1918
Heading	Confidential. Vol 42 War Diary 9th Battn (Hrs) The Royal Scots From 1-9-18 to 30.9.18			
War Diary	Line		01/09/1918	08/09/1918
War Diary	Mazingarbe		09/09/1918	14/09/1918
War Diary	Line		15/09/1918	20/09/1918
War Diary	Vermelles		21/09/1918	22/09/1918
War Diary	Line		23/09/1918	28/09/1918
War Diary	Vermelles		29/09/1918	09/10/1918
War Diary	Line		10/10/1918	11/10/1918
Heading	Vol 45 War Diary 9th Battn (Hrs) The Royal Scots October 1918 Vol 45			
War Diary	Vendin Le Vieil		12/10/1918	15/10/1918

War Diary	Epinoy 9 Carvin	16/10/1918	16/10/1918
War Diary	Esteville. Ref Map Sheet 44A 1/40000	17/10/1918	17/10/1918
War Diary	Wahagnies	18/10/1918	18/10/1918
War Diary	Thouars	19/10/1918	19/10/1918
War Diary	Mouchin	20/10/1918	20/10/1918
War Diary	Basse Rue	21/10/1918	26/10/1918
War Diary	Line	27/10/1918	29/10/1918
War Diary	Deroderie	30/10/1918	31/10/1918
Operation(al) Order(s)	Operation Order No. 30 9th October 1918	09/10/1918	09/10/1918
Operation(al) Order(s)	Operation Order No. 31 9th October 1918	09/10/1918	09/10/1918
Operation(al) Order(s)	Operation Order No. 32 9th October 1918	09/10/1918	09/10/1918
Operation(al) Order(s)	Operation Order No. 32 10th October 1918	10/10/1918	10/10/1918
Operation(al) Order(s)	Operation Order No 33	19/10/1918	19/10/1918
War Diary	OO No 34 Ref Maps Sheet No-37 244 1/40000	21/10/1918	21/10/1918
Operation(al) Order(s)	Operation Orders Ref Map 44 N.W. 1/20000	15/10/1918	15/10/1918
Heading	Volume 46 Confidential War Diary 9th Battn (Hrs.) The Royal Scots. From-1.11.18. to 30.11.18 Vol 46		
War Diary	Deroderie	01/11/1918	08/11/1918
War Diary	Basse Rue	09/11/1918	09/11/1918
War Diary	Jollain Merlin Hollain	09/11/1918	09/11/1918
War Diary	Pipaix	10/11/1918	10/11/1918
War Diary	Ervaux Blicquy. Ormeignies	11/11/1918	11/11/1918
War Diary	Ormeignies	12/11/1918	15/11/1918
War Diary	Tongres Notre Dame	16/11/1918	23/11/1918
War Diary	Attre Mevergnies	24/11/1918	30/11/1918
Operation(al) Order(s)	Operation Order No 36. Reference Maps Sheet 44.1/40,000	08/11/1918	08/11/1918
Operation(al) Order(s)	Operation Order No. 37 Reference Maps. Sheet 44. 1/40,000	09/11/1918	09/11/1918
Operation(al) Order(s)	Operation Order No. 38	10/11/1918	10/11/1918
Operation(al) Order(s)	Operation Order No. 39	11/11/1918	11/11/1918
Operation(al) Order(s)	Operation Order No. 41	23/11/1918	23/11/1918
Heading	War Diary 9th Bn (Hrs) The Royal Scots From 1st Dec 1918 To 31Dec 1918 Volume No. 47		
Miscellaneous	Cover for Documents. Nature of Enclosures.		
War Diary	Attre & Mevergnies	01/12/1918	15/12/1918
War Diary	Soignies	16/12/1918	16/12/1918
War Diary	Tubize	17/12/1918	17/12/1918
War Diary	Braine L'Alleud	08/12/1918	31/12/1918
Operation(al) Order(s)	Operation Order No. 42	05/12/1918	05/12/1918
Operation(al) Order(s)	Operation Order No. 43	15/12/1918	15/12/1918
Heading	War Diary		
Operation(al) Order(s)	Operation Order NO. 44	16/12/1918	16/12/1918
Operation(al) Order(s)	Operation Order No. 45	17/12/1918	17/12/1918
Miscellaneous	9th. Bn. Highrs. The Royal Scots		
Heading	Volume 47. Confidential War Diary 9th Battn (Hrs) The Royal Scots From 1.1.19 to 31.1.19		
Miscellaneous	Cover for Documents. Nature of Enclosures.		
War Diary	Braine L'Alleud	01/01/1919	31/01/1919
War Diary	Braine L'Alleud	27/01/1919	27/01/1919
Heading	Confidential Vol 49 War Diary 9th Battn (Hrs) The Royal Scots. From 1-2-19. to 28.2.19 Vol 49		
Miscellaneous	Cover for Documents. Nature of Enclosures.		
War Diary	Braine L'Alleud	01/02/1919	28/02/1919

Heading	Volume No:- 50. Confidential War Diary 9th Bn (Highlanders) The Royal Scots. From March 1st 1919 to. March 31st 1919 Vol 50		
War Diary	Cover for Documents. Nature of Enclosures.		
War Diary	Braine L'Alleud	01/03/1919	05/03/1919
War Diary	Tubize	06/03/1919	31/03/1919
Heading	Volume 51. Confidential War Diary 9th Battn. (Hrs) The Royal Scots. From 1.4.19. to 30.4.19		
War Diary	Tubize Belgium	01/04/1919	30/04/1919
Heading	Volume 52 Confidential War Diary 9th Battn (Hrs) The Royal Scots. From-1.5.19. to 31.5.19		
War Diary	Tubize	01/05/1919	31/05/1919

Woods 11/25/11

15TH DIVISION
46TH ~~DIVISION~~ BRIGADE

9TH BN ROYAL SCOTS REGT
~~JUN~~ FEB 1918 - MAY 1919

FROM 51 DIV
154 Bde

Attached {
61ST DIVISION
183RD INFY BDE

9TH BN ROYAL SCOTS
FEB — MAY
~~FEB-MAR~~ 1918

Confidential   W 36

War Diary

9th Battn (R.) The Royal Scots

From 1st February 1918   To 28th February 1918

(6339)   Wt. W160/M3016 1,500,000 10/17   McA & W Ltd   (E 1898)   Forms W3091.
Army Form W.3091.

Cover for Documents.

Nature of Enclosures.

Notes, or Letters written.

REF. MAPS. FRANCE 5½ 1/40 000
AMIENS 17 1/20 000
ST QUENTIN 18 1/20 000

9th BN (H.L.I.) THE ROYAL SCOTS. Army Form C. 2118.

WAR DIARY
or
INTELLIGENCE SUMMARY.
(Erase heading not required.)

Instructions regarding War Diaries and Intelligence Summaries are contained in F. S. Regs., Part II. and the Staff Manual respectively. Title pages will be prepared in manuscript.

Place	Date	Hour	Summary of Events and Information	Remarks and references to Appendices
BAILLEULVAL	1.2.18		Battn training in attack.	100F
BAILLEULVAL to COURCELLES LE COMTE	2.2.18		Battn moved from BAILLEULVAL to COURCELLES LE COMTE (No 3 CAMP) — arriving at 11.30 am.	100F
COURCELLES	3.2.18		Church Parade 11.30 am.	100F
do	4.2.18		Battn training in attack. Weather fine.	100F
do	5.2.18		Battn training in attack. The G.O.C. 9th Bgde Kaled farewell to the Officers at Batt Hq.	100F
do	6.2.18		Battn left COURCELLES at 9.00 am and proceeded by road via ACHIET-LE-GRAND BAPAUME & PERONNE to CURENT. 9 Lry ranks) arrived at ETRUM, thought moved by road to BERNELENCOURT. Batt complete in billets 2.30 am	100F
CURENT	7.2.18		Coys engaged in platoon exercises and informing camp examinations.	W.F
	8.2.18		Coys engaged in platoon exercises and informing camp examinations. Battn left CURENT to DOIGNT	100F
	9.2.18		Battn left CURCHY at 8.30 am and marched to VESLES, VOYENNES MATIGNY and DEVINE CAMBRONNE. Complete in billets at 3.30pm. Thought mounted on 2 TRAILLERS. Battn relieved 6 th and 6 Bay	100F
GERMAINE	10.2.18		Coys left GERMAINE at 5.30 am and marched up the night L.R. to 1/4 LONA Trenches on the left, and 3rd Garrison on the right. 1 Coy relief at 07.75 Corps N.H. Kars, and 3 rCo upon 6thing R.Irish Rifles. Relief completed by 9 am	100F
	11.2.18		Moved 1 central Lune of 17 h.L.I.	100F

Army Form C. 2118.

WAR DIARY
or
INTELLIGENCE SUMMARY.
(Erase heading not required.)

Instructions regarding War Diaries and Intelligence Summaries are contained in F. S. Regs., Part II. and the Staff Manual respectively. Title pages will be prepared in manuscript.

Place	Date	Hour	Summary of Events and Information	Remarks and references to Appendices
LINE	12.2.18		Working on defensive Battle Zone.	
"	13.2.18		Do	
"	14.2.18		Do	
"	15.2.18		Relieved 5th Gordons. B & C front two Coys, A counter-attack coy, and D Reserve Coy in FRESNOY. Relief completed by 11.5 p.m.	
"	16.2.18		Working.	
"	17.2.18		Do	
"	18.2.18		Do	
"	19.2.18		Inter-coy relief. A & D relieve B & C. Relief completed 8.10 p.m.	
"	20.2.18		Relatively quiet. Weather fine but very cold.	
"	21.2.18		Do	
"	22.2.18		Bn. relieved by 5th GORDONS & 3/4th OXFORDS, & proceeded to billets at BEAUVOIS. Relief complete 9.30 p.m.	
BEAUVOIS	23.2.18		Echelon B joined the Batn. Completion held to him 23.2.18. Batn engaged in cleaning up after coming out of the line.	
"	24.2.18		Church Parade 10 a.m. Bn. engaged in improvement of billets.	
"	25.2.18		Batn. ch. parade 9 a.m. B.G. engaged in Coy training on improvements billets. B.G engaged working on ?s Cable at ABILLY.	

Army Form C. 2118.

WAR DIARY
or
INTELLIGENCE SUMMARY.
(Erase heading not required.)

Instructions regarding War Diaries and Intelligence Summaries are contained in F. S. Regs., Part II. and the Staff Manual respectively. Title pages will be prepared in manuscript.

Place	Date	Hour	Summary of Events and Information	Remarks and references to Appendices
BEAUVOIS	26.2.18		A, C & D Coys engaged in company training. B Coy covering party at ATTILY. C Coy and two Platoons of D Coy at baths in afternoon.	W.T.
"	27.2.18		C Coy supplied a working party to carry out burying of cable at ATTILY. A & D Coys engaged in Coy training. B Coy at baths. A Coy & two Platoons of D Coy at baths in afternoon.	W.T.
"	28.2.18		Batt'n opened the Battn Zone Defences & thereafter manned out a thin two trench system. 12th O.P. firmed during the night.	W.T.

B. Greenwood

Wt. W4973 M687 750,000 8/16 D. D. & L. Ltd. Forms/C.2118/13.

SECRET   Copy No. 10

OPERATION ORDER NO. 145

REFERENCE MAPS:
Sheet 57.C. 1/20,000
LENS.11. 1/100,000

1. **MOVE:** The Battalion will move to COURCELLES-LE-COMTE tomorrow. (No. 3 Camp)

2. **STARTING TIME:** 9 a.m.

3. **STARTING POINT:** Corner of Main Street W.4.a.20.99

4. **ORDER OF MARCH:** H.Q., B.C.D.A Companies and Transport. 200 yards between Battalions and 100 yards between Companies. Pipers with Companies.

5. **ROUTE:** BELLACOURT - RANSART - ADINFER - AYETTE.

6. **BLANKETS AND STORES:** Officers valises, blankets canteen and signalling stores will be stacked at Orderly Room by 8 a.m. Mess stores will be packed and ready by 8.15 a.m. and will be called for by Mess Cart.

7. **ADVANCE PARTY:** Lieut. T.D.H. LAWSON and 1 N.C.O. per Company will proceed to COURCELLES-LE-COMTE and take over No. 3 Camp

8. **DRESS:** Full marching order - Steel helmets strapped on packs - Leather jerkins will be worn.

ACKNOWLEDGE:

Issued at ..... p.m.

Capt &A/Adjt.
9th. Royal Scots.

1st. February, 1918.

Copy No. 1 to O.C. A Coy   Copy No. 7 to M.O.
"   "   2 " O.C. B "   "   "   8 " Specialist Officers
"   "   3 " O.C. C "   "   "   9 " Lieut. LAWSON
"   "   4 " O.C. D "   "   " 10 " War Diary ✓
"   "   5 " Q.M.   "   " 11 " Adjutant
"   "   6 " T.O.   "   " 12 " File

SECRET: Copy No. 10

OPERATION ORDERS NO. 146.

Reference Maps:
Sheet 57.C.1/20,000
LENS.11.,1/100,000
AMIENS.17.1/100,000

1.	MOVE:	The Battalion will move by bus to CURCHY on 6th. February – Transport by road.
2.	STARTING TIME:	8.40 a.m.
3.	STARTING POINT:	A.18.a.35.10.
4.	ORDER OF MARCH:	Companies will march to the embussing point in the following order:- B.,A.,D.,C.,H.Q.
5.	ROUTE:	ACHIET-LE-GRAND, - BAPAUME, - PERONNE - CURCHY.
6.	BLANKETS AND STORES:	Officers valises, one blanket per man, canteen Orderly Room and Signal Stores will be stacked outside Q.M.Stores by 8 a.m.
7.	DRESS:	Full marching order. One blanket per man will be carried rolled on the top of the pack. Greatcoats will be worn. A haversack ration will be carried by each man.
8.	GENERAL:	One Cook per Company will remain with cooker and come on with Transport. Remainder of cooks will accompany the Company on the busses. Camp kettles will be carried on motor lorries.
9.	TRANSPORT:	Transport will move by road - Staging areas are as follows:- 6th. February............BEAULENCOURT. 7th. " ....DOINGT 8th. " ....CURCHY Billets for the 6th. and 7th. will be allotted by the respective Town Majors.
10.	STARTING TIME:	9 a.m.
11.	ROUTE:	First Day:- ACHIET-LE-GRAND, - BAPAUME - BEAULENCOURT. Second Day:- RANCOURT, - PERONNE, - DOINGT. Third Day:- LE MESNIL, - ST.CHRIST, - LICOURT POTTE, - CURCHY.

ACKNOWLEDGE:

Issued at ... 1.45 ... p.m.   Capt & A/Adjt.
                                                                      6th. Royal Scots.

5TH. FEBRUARY, 1918.

```
Copy No. 1 to O.C. A Coy        Copy No. 7 to M.O.
  "    "  2  "  O.C. B  "         "    "   8  "  Specialist Offrs.
  "    "  3  "  O.C. C  "         "    "   9  "  War Diary
  "    "  4  "  O.C. D  "         "    "  10  "  Adjutant
  "    "  5  "  Q.M.              "    "  11  "  File
  "    "  6  "  T.O.
```

SECRET:

Copy No. 10

OPERATION ORDER NO.147:

REFERENCE MAPS:-
AMIENS. 1/100,000
ST.QUENTIN. 1/100,000

1. **MOVE:** The Battalion will move to GERMAINE tomorrow. Transport Lines and Q.M.Stores to ETREILLERS and take over from 4th. Gloucesters.

2. **STARTING TIME:** 9.30 a.m.

3. **STARTING POINT:** Cross Roads at C in CURCHY.

4. **ORDER OF MARCH:** H.Q., D.A.B.C. Companies and Transport.

5. **ROUTE:** NESLE, - VOYENNES, - MATIGNY, - DOUILLY, - GERMAINE.

6. **BLANKETS AND STORES:** Officers valises, blankets, Canteen and Signalling Stores will be stacked outside Q.M.Stores by 8 a.m. Mess Stores will be packed and ready by 8.45 a.m. and will be called for by Mess Cart.

7. **ADVANCE PARTY:** Lieut. T.D.H.LAWSON and one N.C.O. per Company will report at Battalion H.Q. at 8 a.m. and proceed by bus and take over billets vacated by 5th. Gordon Highrs.

8. **DRESS:** Full Marching Order - Steel Helmets strapped on packs.

9. **GENERAL:**
   (i) Leather jerkins will be rolled inside Company blankets.
   (ii) Transport: A distance of 25 yards will be left between every 6 vehicles.

ACKNOWLEDGE:

8th. FEBRUARY, 1918:

Issued at..........p.m.

[signature]
Capt & A/Adjt.
6th. Royal Scots.

```
Copy No. 1 to O.C. A Coy      Copy No. 7 to M.O.
  "    "  2 "  O.C. B  "        "    "  8 "  Specialist Officers
  "    "  3 "  O.C. C  "        "    "  9 "  Lieut. T.D.H.LAWSON
  "    "  4 "  O.C. D  "        "    " 10 "  War Diary
  "    "  5 "  Q.M.             "    " 11 "  Adjutant ✓
  "    "  6 "  T.O.             "    " 12 "  File
```

SECRET: Copy No. 8

OPERATION ORDER NO. 148:

Reference Maps:
Sheet 62.C.S.E.
Sheet 66.D.N.E.
Sheet 62.B.S.W.

1. **RELIEF:** The 9th.Royal Scots will relieve the 2/7th.Warwicks on the Left and 2/8 Warwicks on Right, in Reserve on the night of 11/12 February, 1918.

2. **DISPOSITION:** "B" & "C" Companies will take over from 3/7th.Warwicks in MAISSEMY. "B" Company taking over from 2 Companies - "C" Company taking over from 1 Company. "A" & "D" Companies will take over from 2/8 Warwicks in OTTER COPSE. "A" Company taking over from 1 Company - "D" Company taking over from 2 Companies.

3. **STARTING TIME:** H.Q., "B" & "C" Companies 2.45 p.m. - "A" & "D" Companies 3.30 p.m.

4. **STARTING POINT:** Cross Roads E.17.b.4.9.

5. **ROUTE:** H.Q., "B" & "C" Companies - VAUX, - ETREILLERS, - ATTILLY, - MARTEVILLE, - VILLECHOLLES, - MAISSEMY.
"A" & "D" Companies - VAUX, - ETREILLERS, - SAVY, - HOLNON, - OTTER COPSE.

6. **BILLETING PARTY:** 1 Officer and 4 men from "B" & "C" Companies and 1 Officer and 4 men from "D" & "A" Companies will report at the respective Battalion H.Q. whom they are relieving to be shown accommodation so as to be able to guide their Companies in.

7. **TRANSPORT:** Transport Lines and Q.M.Stores will remain at ETREILLERS.

8. **LEWIS GUNS:** Lewis Gun limbers will accompany their respective Companies. "B" Company cooker and 1 Water Cart for 2 Left Companies - "A" Company cooker and 1 water cart for 2 Right Companies.

9. **TRENCH STORES:** Trench Stores will be taken over and lists sent to Battalion H.Q. by 9 a.m. on 12th.inst. Gum boots will not be taken over.

10. **COMPLETION OF RELIEF:** On completion of relief - code word - "Company Commanders surname" will be wired to Battalion H.Q.

11. **ECHELON "B":** Echelon "B" under command of Captain W.R.RICHARD will be responsible for cleaning up the billets and will proceed to Transport Lines half-an-hour after departure of last Company. Certificate of cleanliness will be obtained from Town Major or representative and forwarded to Battalion Orderly Room by 6 p.m. on 12th.

ACKNOWLEDGE:

Issued at........p.m.

10th FEBRUARY, 1918:

Capt & A/Adjt.
9th.Royal Scots.

Copy No.1 to O.C. A Coy
"   "   2 " O.C. B "
"   "   3 " O.C. C "
"   "   4 " O.C. D "
"   "   5 " Q.M.
"   "   6 " T.O.
"   "   7 " M.O.

Copy No. 8 to Specialist Officers
"   "   9 " O.C. 2/7 Warwicks
"   " 10 " O.C. 2/8 Warwicks
"   " 11 " War Diary
"   " 12 " Adjutant
"   " 13 " File

ADDENDUM TO OPERATION ORDER NO. 148.

12. **Order of March:** Companies will march at 200 Yards interval up to MARTEVILLE and HOLNON. After that point 100 yards between platoons.

AMENDMENT TO OPERATION ORDER NO. 148.

Para. 4. **Starting Point:** Starting Point is E.17.b.8.8. and not as stated.

11th February, 1918.

Capt & A/Adjt.
9th. Royal Scots.

Copies to all recipients of O.O. No. 148.

SECRET   Copy No. 12

OPERATION ORDER No 149

Map References
    Sheet 62 B S.W. 1/20,000
    "   62 C S.E. 1/20,000

1. **RELIEF** The Battalion will relieve the 5° Gordon Hrs in the right subsector of the Brigade front on night of 13/14th Inst.

2. **DISPOSITIONS**
    B Coy on Right Front relieving A Coy of 5° Gordon Hrs
    C " " Left Front boy relieving B Coy of 5° Gordon Hrs
    A " " Crumble Attack boy relieving C Coy of 5° Gordon Hrs
    D " " TRESNOY DEFENCE relieving D Coy of 5° Gordon Hrs

3. **ROUTE** B & C Coys R.31.b.0.2. thence by track to M.26.d.9.9 (approx mark) This route must be reconnoitred before hand.
    A & D Coys — Road to M.26.d.9.9.

4. **GUIDES** Guides will meet Coys at M.26.d.9.9 as follows — one per platoon for Crumble attack and a TRESNOY STRONG POINT Coy. One per sect for front line coys. Guides will be in possession of a slip stating Coy, platoon and posts for which they are guides.

5. **STARTING TIME**   6 P.M.

2

6. RATIONS   Ration dumps are as follows:—
   For Bn HQ – M.26.d.9.4.
   Left Front Coy – GRICOURT M.22.d.9.7.
   Right Front Coy – MOUNT NEEDLE M.34.d.
   Right 2 platoons (Counter attack Coy)
   "   2   "   Reserve Coy.   } MOUNT NEEDLE
   Left 2   "   Counter attack Coy } FRESNOY CRATER
   "   2   "   Reserve Coy   } M.27.b.5.7
   O.C. Coys will leave parties to bring up
   rations from their dumps to the Coys.

7. ADVANCE PARTY   2 HQ Signallers
                   1 Signaller per Coy
                   5 Runners per Coy
                   1 Bn HQ runner per Coy
   These will report at HQ 5th Gordon Hrs at 3 p.m.
   on 15th Inst and learn there way about.

8. TRENCH STORES   Trench stores will be taken
   over and duplicate copies forwarded to Bn
   HQ by 9AM on morning after relief.

9. Relief complete will be reported to Bn HQ
   by code word – GILLETTE

   Acknowledge

Issued at   pm   Capt Adjt
16.2.18   9th Royal Scots

3.

DISTRIBUTION

Copy No 1 to OC A Coy
"   " 2 "   B "
"   " 3 "   C "
"   " 4 "   D "
"   " 5 " OC 5th Gordon Hos
"   " 6 " Lio Sect
"   " 7 " O.M.
"   " 8 " T.O.
"   " 9 " C.O.
"   " 10 " Adjt
"   " 11 " WAR DIARY

SECRET   OPERATION ORDER   G. Clegg
                No. 60
Pt of 62E SW
  62° SE

1. RELIEF Inter Company relief will take place
           tomorrow Aug 6 19/20th Inst
           D Coy relieving C Coy
           A "   "   B Coy
           Relieving Coy will not start before 6pm

2. GUIDES One guide per pt will be supplied by
           B & C Coys and meet corresponding Pt
           of D & A Coy at a point to be chosen by
           Coy Commanders. D & A Coys will
           leave behind 1 officer per Coy and
           one man per platoon to hand over
           to relieving platoons of B & C Coys
           After relief rear parties of D & A Coys
           will rejoin their respective platoons.

3. TRENCH STORES All trench stores will be handed
           over and receipts obtained
           Duplicate copies of stores handed
           over will be sent to Battn HQ
           not more than 24 hours after relief

4. LEWIS GUNS On relief C Coy will hand over 1 Lewis Gun
           and ammunition to D Coy. B Coy will
           hand over one Lewis Gun and
           ammunition to A Coy.

Relief completed & reported to
Batt. H.Q. ca CODEWORD ELGIN

Sawent   T.W. Pauline
18.3.18   Lt/Adjt
                              ROGER

Copies may 1 O.C. Coy
        2   B "
        3   C
        4   D
        5   OM
        6   TO
        7   QM
        8   7b
        9   War Diary

SECRET   OPERATION ORDER   COPY N°9
No 151

Ref Sh 62B SW 7 1/20,000
       62C SE 5

1. MOVE On night 20/21st Batn HQ will close
at Quarry M.27.c.05 at 6 p.m. and
open at HQrs of 1/5th Batn
M.27.A.4.4. at same hour

2. Platoon in CORN WOOD will move at
5.45 p.m. to previously selected position.
An officer will report to Bn HQ at 10 A.M.
to be shown positions. One officer
will remain behind to hand over to
5th Gordons.

3. Platoons in CORN WOOD will not hand
over picks & shovels received from R boys
but will carry them to their new positions

4. Mining Platoon will move into shelters
near CARTENAY WOOD during
afternoon 20th

5. TRENCH STORES Trench stores will be handed
over and receipts taken

Acknowledge

Issued midnight
19-2-18

H. Carter
Capt & Adjt
R.D.B.B.

DISTRIBUTION

Copy No 1 O.C. "A" Coy
"   " 2   "B"
"   " 3   "C"
"   " 4   "D"
"   " 5   Q.M
"   " 6   T.O.
"   " 7   Adjt
"   " 8   File
"   " 9   War Diary

SECRET   OPERATION ORDER No 152   COPY No
                                                                 O.O.
REF. MAPS.   60 B SW 1/20,000
             62 C SE 1/20,000

1. RELIEF   The Battalion will be relieved on the night 22/23rd by the 5th Gordons
                  on left and 4th Oxfords on right and will move to BEAUVOIS

2.   At 2pm tomorrow the following adjustment will be made:- 2 Platoons
                  B Coy at present in GRICOURT will come under command of OC. D Coy.
                  Posts 9 & 10 will come under command of OC. A Coy.
                  These adjustments will hold until arrival in BEAUVOIS after relief
                  OC. Coys taking over command of fresh posts will detail necessary
                  guides and are responsible that the trench stores in these posts are
                  handed over and receipts obtained.

3. DISPOSITIONS   D Coy 5th Gordons will take over posts 15, 16, 17 from D Coy 9th Royal Scots
                  C Coy 5th Gordons will take over posts 11, 12, 13 & 14 from D Coy 9th Royal Scots
                  Guides 1 per post at D Coy HQrs GRICOURT, M.22.a.8.9. at 6 pm
                  C Coy 5th Gordons will take over from the 2 platoons B Coy 9th Royal Scots under
                  command of OC D Coy in GRICOURT.
                  1 Guide per platoon from B Coy to be at D Coy HQ. M.22.a.8.9. at 6 pm
                  B Coy 5th Gordons will relieve C Coy 9th Royal Scots in FRESNOY STRONG POINT
                  Guides 1 per platoon to be at crater M.27.c.3.6. at 5.30 pm
                  C Coy Oxfords will take over posts 1, 2, 3, 4 & 9A (L.G. post) from A Coy 9th Royal Scots
                  B Coy Oxfords will take over posts 5, 6, 7, 8, 9 & 10 from A Coy 9th Royal Scots
                  Guides 1 per post & 1 per Coy HQrs to be at MONT NEEDLE, M.36.b.4.1. at 7.30 PM
                  1 Officer & n.c.o. of C Coy Oxfords will take over stores by midday
                  sending their own guides for reserve platoons
                  Guides at the MONT NEEDLE 1 per post & 1 per Coy HQrs. Guides for 9 & 10 posts
                  will report to HQ A Coy and proceed to NEEDLE with A Coy guides
                  Counter Attack Platoon of B Coy at A Coy HQrs and Reserve Platoon of A Coy
                  will be assembled in AMBOISE TRENCH by 7pm and will move
                  out as soon as Reserve platoons are reported in position and
                  relief of A Coy complete

4. TRENCH STORES Trench Maps & Trench Stores will be handed over and receipts obtained in
                  duplicate

5. BILLETING PARTY Coy QMSs will take over billets in BEAUVOIS from Town Major by 5pm on
                  22nd and arrange to guide their Coys in on relief

6. ROUTE   Track KEEPERS HOUSE – MARTEVILLE – VILLEVEQUE – BEAUVOIS
                  All movement to be by platoons at 100 yards interval

7. RELIEF COMPLETE Relief complete will be wired to Bn. HQ.
                        A Coy   CODE WORD   OFFICERS 1
                        B   do   do   2
                        C   do   do   3
                        D   do   do   4

                                                          J.W. Rawlin
                                                          Capt & Adjt
                                         9th Royal Scots

Issued at   PM
 21.2.18

                                                                   P.T.O.

DISTRIBUTION
Copy No 1   O C A Coy
  "   " 2   B "
  "   " 3   C "
  "   " 4   D "
  "   " 5   C O 5th Gordon Hrs
  "   " 6   Q.M.
  "   " 7   T.O.
  "   " 8   ADJT.
  "   " 9   File
  "   " 10   War Diary

Army Form C. 2118

9th Battalion (new) The Royal Scots

WAR DIARY
or
INTELLIGENCE SUMMARY
(Erase heading not required.)

Instructions regarding War Diaries and Intelligence Summaries are contained in F. S. Regs., Part II. and the Staff Manual respectively. Title Pages will be prepared in manuscript.

March 1918

Place	Date	Hour	Summary of Events and Information	Remarks and references to Appendices
Estrouars	1.3.18		Battalion in Training.	W.P.S.
"	2.3.18		Battalion relieved 5th Gordon Hrs in the line B Coy Left front, C Coy Right D Coy Reserve by A Coy counter attack Coy. Echelon B moved to billets in Villevèque	Q.P.S.
Line	3.3.18		Battalion in line. Line very quiet. Nothing of interest happened	Q.P.S.
Do	4.3.18		Do	Q.P.S.
Do	5.3.18		Do	Q.P.S.
Do	6.3.18		Do	Q.P.S.
Do	7.3.18		Do	Q.P.S.
Do	8.3.18		Do	Q.P.S.
Do	9.3.18		Do	Q.P.S.
Do	10.3.18		Battalion relieved by 8th A.S.H. Battalion thereafter marched to billets at Marcville	Q.P.S.
Marcville	11.3.18		Battalion engaged in various parties in Battle Zone	Q.P.S.
Do	12.3.18		Do	Q.P.S.
Do	13.3.18		Do	Q.P.S.
Do	14.3.18		Do	Q.P.S.
Do	15.3.18		Do	Q.P.S.
Do	16.3.18		Do	Q.P.S.
Do	17.3.18		Do	Q.P.S.
Do	18.3.18		Do	Q.P.S.
Do	19.3.18		Battalion left Marcville at 4 p.m. and marched to Beauvois and left on concentration zone led by 5th Gordon H's.	Q.P.S.
Beauvois	20.3.18		Battalion engaged on Coy and specialist training	Q.P.S.
"	21.3.18		at 5.30 am orders to man Battle position received. Battalion left Beauvois a certain number of Battery and took up Battle Coys A.B.C. and stated accordingly throughout the day.	Q.P.S.

1875 Wt. W593/826 1,000,000 4/15 J.B.C. & A. A.D.S.S./Forms/C. 2118.

Army Form C. 2118.

WAR DIARY
or
INTELLIGENCE SUMMARY.
(Erase heading not required.)

Instructions regarding War Diaries and Intelligence Summaries are contained in F. S. Regs., Part II. and the Staff Manual respectively. Title pages will be prepared in manuscript.

Place	Date	Hour	Summary of Events and Information	Remarks and references to Appendices
LINE	22.3.18		Reliefs Coys and Reserve Platoon, especially C. About 11 a.m. Battalion was ordered to be prepared to move	
			6 C.S.M. in Battle Zone. At 12.30 pm ordered to withdraw to VAUDRICOURT C Coy covering the withdrawal	
			Batn. arr. abt 10.30 pm ordered to withdraw to & cover front of BOUVINES C Coy expected up to join headquarters	
			2 Officers and about 38 men being B.O. the next being left 2, 3 Coys in left of A & B Coys in left of centre companies 9s Sisters	
			Lt. a Co. G.A.Stiff, also 2nd & 3rd Lieutenants after extra men of platoons Lt. MacTurk, E. Murca	G.R.S.
P.	23.3.18		Posn. ordered to withdraw and march to VAUXRIEUX which were subsequently carried out, 6.7.30 am abt 3.30 am	
			about march to N22. Shortly after ordered to CONSERVOIR and Batt. finally housed in BROUX & BOUCOUL	
			with B Coy remainder of Battalion in CONSERVOIR. Battalion withdrew to N22 in course 2	G.R.S.
Do.	24.3.18		At 9 a.m ordered forward from N22 front line MERE & MERIS St. NICOIS & BRAYEUX to be in Battle with the Brigade	
			in Support. Notes being lined Kaiga Contre. abt 12 noon Brigade lifted up at 12.30 pm ordered to withdraw	
			toward front but eventually to Skoppin in front of MESNIL Battalion was relieved and withdrew to Mesnil	
			by 2nd Divis. Battalion filed S.of. in line MESNIL- BOIS Battalion in Gr G.S.R.M. withdrew to D.H.Q. at night	G.R.S.
Do.	25.3.18		Early morning 2 L.T. Bottelan. Battalion gained brown and defence about 300 yds East of Nesnil near BATHLEMONT	
			HALLU. in Case of German attack. Kaiga 1827. Was to make a counter attack by 2nd Linconlins at present there is	
			Battn. An Battalion in support. in orders to RETREVILLES on JUSSY to TURGETTE the Bth Pioneers 1841.Fentreled on arrival	
			There orders passed to Lt. QUESNEL and Adjn. DUNCAN	G.R.S.

WAR DIARY or INTELLIGENCE SUMMARY

Army Form C. 2118.

Place	Date	Hour	Summary of Events and Information	Remarks and references to Appendices
LE QUESNOY	25.3.18		Battalion relieved forward to BERNICOURT. On arrival reports were found that one Battalion with 2/5 & W Green & 2 DSO 5th Royal Sussex supplying two Coys 3rd & 4th and Coy 8th RS Head Coy Battalion took up defensive line West of BERNICOURT. Orders to move from BERNICOURT & join a Bn of 14 Gallipoli outside main road.	A.Q.S.
LINE	27.3.18		Battalion moved forward to MOREUIL to take up line 2nd ave SW of village. A Coy of village Battalion observed by enemy about midnight 27/28	A.Q.S.
"	28.3.18		Battalion passed by bus to MOREUILCOURT. On arrival at MORISCOVE about 5am prepared to support a counter attack on MOREUIL	A.Q.S.
		6.30 am	ordered to move into position N of railway and S.W of LAMOTTE. A Company was ordered to occupy the village Coy advanced to within 200 yds of village but was stopped by heavy fire. Many men wounded. a° 3rd 5 platoons of D Company S.Q Moreuil ave and back supporting	A.Q.S.
	29.3.18		Battalion H.Q. moved before daylight to N of WOOD E of VILLERS BRETONNEUX – AUBERCOURT ROAD. Situation intermittent.	A.Q.S.
	30.3.18		Heavy German attack on troops on right of Battalion. Enemy appeared to be pushing his way into battalion lines and K.O. up position in wood West of Coys of Australians came up to carry out counter attack. On enemy counter attack. Enemy coming to battalion was driven back. Ordered was rued to support battalion now advanced midnight of 30/31 as marched to CAYEUX.	A.Q.S.
CAYEUX	31.3.18		Battalion remained at CAYEUX to rally. Few killed. Battalion moved to neighboring field and stoved to billets in CAYEUX for the night.	
			Losses 15th officers 287 o.r. wounded 6 offrs 138 o.r. missing 2 offrs 94 Shellshock concussion 2 o.r. 38 O.R. Killed 7 o.r. Died of wounds	A.Q.S.

John D. Muir Lieut Col
Comdg 9th R.S. (Glasgow) H.C R.S.

183rd Brigade.

61st Division.

1/9th BATTALION

THE ROYAL SCOTS REGIMENT

APRIL 1918.

REF MAPS. FRANCE. AMIENS. 17. V/100,000.
FRANCE. HAZEBROUCK. 5A/100,000.

WAR DIARY or **INTELLIGENCE SUMMARY**
(Erase heading not required.)

9th Bn (H.Rs) The Royal Scots April 1918 183

Army Form C. 2118

Instructions regarding War Diaries and Intelligence
Summaries are contained in F.S. Regs., Part II.
and the Staff Manual respectively. Title Pages
will be prepared in manuscript.

Place	Date	Hour	Summary of Events and Information	Remarks and references to Appendices
GENTELLES	1-4-18		Battalion took up position on the c/um NW of Gentelles. Moved into trenches in afternoon S.E. of village.	A.Q.S.
LINE.	2-4-18		Battalion remained in same position throughout the day 3-4-18 and then drawn to BRIQUEMESNIL arriving 5-30 a.m. 3-4-18.	A.Q.S.
BRIQUEMESNIL	3-4-18		Marched to VERGIES where battalion went to billets.	A.Q.S.
VERGIES	4-4-18		Battalion spent the day cleaning up.	A.Q.S.
Do	5-4-18		Training was carried out.	A.Q.S.
Do	6-4-18		Draft arrived 328.	A.Q.S.
Do	7-4-18		Training	A.Q.S.
Do	8-4-18		Do	A.Q.S.
Do	9-4-18		Do	A.Q.S.
Do	10-4-18		Battalion marched to Hangest-sur-Somme, where it entrained for Merville, area de-training at STEENBECQUE at 1-30 p.m. 11-4-18.	A.Q.S.
STEENBECQUE	11-4-18		Received orders from G.O.C. at 4 p.m., battalion on fighting kit by 4-20 p.m. and marched to line between O5a20 to O3b50. B.C.D & A Coys in support. Bn. H.Q. K32.D.7.1. Battalion entered front to left at 11-5 p.m.	A.Q.S.

REF MAPS. FRANCE AMIENS 1/7 100,000
FRANCE HAZEBROUCK 5A 40,000

WAR DIARY or INTELLIGENCE SUMMARY

Army Form C. 2118.

9th Bn H^{rs} The Royal Scots

Instructions regarding War Diaries and Intelligence Summaries are contained in F.S. Regs., Part II. and the Staff Manual respectively. Title pages will be prepared in manuscript.

(Erase heading not required.)

Place	Date	Hour	Summary of Events and Information	Remarks and references to Appendices
LINE	12-4-18		51st Division withdrew between 6.20 and 8 am. Gordons fell back at 7 am. Bn. HQ changed at 8.15 am and late at 12.0 pm. Enemy of 13th arranged to take up position in J.35a. At 11 p.m. order received and Battalion moved to billets in ST VENANT. Bombard Bn. made ellay ellois 9/R.S. including 2 Coys of the 9/R.S. was formed.	G.O.S
ST. VENANT	13-4-18		Battalion stood to at 5 am and at 8 am. Bn. HQ were ordered to man trenches in Rd at 10 a.m. How. Bn. made up and Bn. HQ & BC.Coy went into cellars in St Venant B.Coy standing fast in the trenches four Coys were organised and 2 of new Battalion moved forward on relieved 2/5 Gloucester Regt.	G.O.S
LINE	14-4-18		Battalion dispositions the same as on 13th with S.Q. at 1 Sqdr on the left and 2/8th Worcesters on the right. Lt. Col. Gunn left to command the 153 Brigade.	G.O.S
Do	15-4-18		Nothing of importance happened. Line quiet.	G.O.S
Do	16-4-18		Do. Lieut Col Mains assumed command of Bn	G.O.S
Do	17-4-18		Nothing of importance happened. Line quiet.	G.O.S
Do	18-4-18		Battalion went into billets in ST VENANT.	G.O.S
Do	19-4-18		Battalion remained in billets.	G.O.S
Do	20-4-18		Battalion took over left sector from 3rd Gordons with two Coys B.Coy in front in support Art Coy in billets	G.O.S

Ref Maps. France. Amiens. 17. 1/100,000
France. Hazebrouck. 5A. 1/100,000

Army Form C. 2118.

WAR DIARY
or
INTELLIGENCE SUMMARY.
(Erase heading not required.)

9TH BNRS THE ROYAL SCOTS.

Instructions regarding War Diaries and Intelligence Summaries are contained in F.S. Regs., Part II. and the Staff Manual respectively. Title pages will be prepared in manuscript.

Place	Date	Hour	Summary of Events and Information	Remarks and references to Appendices
LINE	21-4-18.		Disposition of Battalion as on 20th.	H.Q.S.
Do.	22-4-18.		C Coy relieved B who went into billets. A Coy reinforced – 3rd Garrison Bn.	H.Q.S.
Do.	23-4-18.		Disposition of Battalion as on 22nd. Sent guide.	H.Q.S.
LINE	24-4-18.		Battalion was relieved by 8th A.& S.H. A Coy enclosed	H.Q.S.
ST VENANT.	25-4-18.		Battalion sent into billets in St Venant.	H.Q.S.
Do.	26-4-18.		Battalion remained in billets in St Venant.	H.Q.S.
LINE	27-4-18.		Relieved 3rd Gordons and 8th A.& S.H. on the night of 27/28th. Bde Orders for this A.C. on offbat him.	H.Q.S.
Do.	28-4-18.		Battalion in the line. Quiet. Nothing of importance reported.	H.Q.S.
Do.	29-4-18.		Do.	H.Q.S.
Do.	30-4-18.		Battalion was relieved on the night of the 30th/1st May by the 3rd Gordons and 8th A.& S.H. and marched to billets outside St Venant.	H.Q.S.
			Drafts. 14 Officers 652 O.Rs.	H.Q.S.
			Estimated Casualties. 1 Officer and 15 O.Rs killed. 7 Officers and 135 O.Rs wounded. 144 O.Rs missing.	H.Q.S.
			2 O.Rs died of wounds.	

John B. Muir Lieut. Col.
Comdg 9th Bn. (H.Q.S.) The R.S.

CONFIDENTIAL.
No. 38

WAR DIARY.

9TH BN. (HRS) THE ROYAL SCOTS

1ST MAY, 1918 — 31ST MAY, 1918.

36 RS.

Reference Maps:— FRANCE SHEET 36 N.E. 1/20,000
D° D° 36 N.E. 1/20,000
HAZEBROUCK 3A 1/100,000

WAR DIARY
INTELLIGENCE SUMMARY

Army Form C. 2118.

9th Batt" (H¹) The Royal Scots

Place	Date	Hour	Summary of Events and Information	Remarks and references to Appendices
AISNE D'AILENNES ST VENANT	1-5-18		Battalion spent day cleaning up, baths &c	A.P.S.
D°	2-5-18		Battalion engaged in Coy Training. Baths. Working parties sent up in evening	A.P.S.
D°	3-5-18		Battalion relieved 5th Gordon H¹rs & 8th A&S H¹rs in the line	A.P.S.
LINE	4-5-18		A Coy Right Front. B Coy Right Support. C Coy Left Front. D Coy Left Support	A.P.S.
D°	5-5-18		Line quiet nothing to report	A.P.S.
D°	6-5-18		D°	A.P.S.
D°	7-5-18		D°	A.P.S.
D°	8-5-18		Battalion was relieved in the line by 5th Gordon H¹rs and 8th A&S H¹rs and thereafter took up Brigade Reserve in billets at AISLES D'AILENNES - ST VENANT	A.P.S.
AISLE D'AILENNES ST VENANT	9-5-18		Battalion spent day cleaning up	A.P.S.
D°	10-5-18		Battalion engaged in Coy Training, Baths &c. Working parties supplied in evening	A.P.S.
D°	11-5-18		D°	A.P.S.
D°	12-5-18		Battalion relieved 5th Gordon H¹rs and 8th A&S H¹rs in line. B Coy Right Front. A Coy Right Support. D Coy Left Front. C Coy Left Support	A.P.S.
LINE	13-5-18		Line quiet nothing to report. Lt Col J.B. Muir D.S.O. proceeded on one months leave. Major R.G. Morrison M.C. 2nd A&S H¹rs assumed command of Battalion	A.P.S.
D°	14-5-18		Line quiet nothing to report	A.P.S.
D°	15-5-18		D°	A.P.S.
D°	16-5-18		Battalion was relieved in line by 5th Gordon H¹rs and 8th A&S H¹rs and thereafter moved into Brigade Reserve at AISLE D'AILENNES - ST VENANT	A.P.S.

WAR DIARY
or
INTELLIGENCE SUMMARY.
(Erase heading not required.)

Army Form C. 2118.

Place	Date	Hour	Summary of Events and Information	Remarks and references to Appendices
ASILE D'HALLENNES ST VENANT	17-5-18		Battalion spent day cleaning up.	
Do	18-5-18		Battalion engaged in Coy training. Working parties supplied in evening.	
Do	19-5-18		Do	
Do	20-5-18		Battalion relieved 5th Gordon Hrs & 8th A. & S. Hrs in the line. A Coy Right Front B Coy Right Support C Coy Left Front D Coy Left Support Coy.	
LINE	21-5-18		Line quiet, nothing to report.	
Do	22-5-18		Do	
Do	23-5-18		Do	
Do	24-5-18		Battalion was relieved in line by 5th Gordon Hrs and 8th A. & S. Hrs and Bandsmen moved into Brigade Reserve	
ASILE D'HALLENNES ST VENANT	25-5-18		in billets ASILE D'HALLENNES - ST VENANT	
Do	26-5-18		Battalion engaged cleaning up.	
Do	27-5-18		Battalion engaged in Coy training Working parties were supplied in evening	
Do	28-5-18		Do	
Do	29-5-18		Do	
Do	30-5-18		Do	
Do	31-5-18		Orders were received to move to ARRAS. Battalion moved in evening to billets in MOLINGHEM	
			During month 81 OR Casualties 3 OR Killed 21 OR wounded. Duffs joined during month A. Gordon transferred to Home Establishment (auth A.S. 2138/2397/9 3-5-18.	

Commanding 7/8th (Hd) The Royal Scots

CONFIDENTIAL

9 Roy Scot
Vol 39

WAR DIARY

Came from 61st 1.6.18

June '18
May '19

37 R.S.

9TH BN (HS) THE ROYAL SCOT

FROM 1ST JUNE — 30TH JUNE

Reference maps :- LENS 11. 1/100,000.
3/S 1/40,000
3/c 1/40,000

3rd Batt" (H/S) The Royal Scots

Army Form C. 2118.

WAR DIARY
or
INTELLIGENCE SUMMARY.
(Erase heading not required.)

Place	Date	Hour	Summary of Events and Information	Remarks and references to Appendices
MOLINGHEM	1.6.18		Battalion marched to AIRE where it entrained for MAROEUIL. Battalion was transferred from 61st & 15th Division. The following officers joined from Div Wing 2/Lt R. MARSHALL, 2/Lt T.H. LAURIE, 2/Lt G.E. BARCLAY, 2/Lt W.M. ROBERTSON, 2/Lt H.D. MACGREGOR.	A.L.
ARRAS	2.6.18		Battalion arrived MAROEUIL at 12.45 a.m. and thereafter marched to ARRAS arriving at 3 a.m. Battalion spent remainder of day cleaning up.	A.L.
ARRAS	3.6.18		Coy Training, Baths and Range.	A.L.
ARRAS	4.6.18		Coy Training, Baths, Range. See Appearance of Battn. Tested in Gas Chamber.	A.L.
ARRAS	5.6.18		Battalion engaged in Coy Training.	A.L.
ARRAS	6.6.18		Battalion moved from ARRAS to WAKEFIELD CAMP. Coys A 2.3.8 and Tpt over Billets from 4/5 Black Watch. Hqrs joined from Staff. 2/Lt A.S. DREW and Lt 9th BN Q.M. J.F. ANDERSON 6th S.R.	A.L.
WAKEFIELD CAMP	7.6.18		Battalion engaged in Coy Training.	A.L.
"	8.6.18		do	A.L.
"	9.6.18		Battalion relieved 11th A & S.H. in the line. Batt H.Q. and 3 Coys in STIRLING CAMP Brigade Reserve. A Coy in ATHIES. Details and Echelon B moved to AGNEZ-LES-DUISANS.	A.L.
"	10.6.18		Line very quiet. Working parties were supplied by Battalion.	A.L.
"	11.6.18		do	A.L.
"	12.6.18		do	A.L.
"	13.6.18		do	A.L.
"	14.6.18		do	A.L.
"	15.6.18		do	A.L.

Army Form C. 2118.

WAR DIARY
or
INTELLIGENCE SUMMARY.
(Erase heading not required.)

Instructions regarding War Diaries and Intelligence Summaries are contained in F.S. Regs., Part II. and the Staff Manual respectively. Title pages will be prepared in manuscript.

Place	Date	Hour	Summary of Events and Information	Remarks and references to Appendices
Lens	16.6.18		Line very quiet, working parties supplied.	A.P.L.
Do	17.6.18		Battalion relieved 10th Scottish Rifles in Left subsector Right Brigade Front. C Coy Right Front Coy, D Coy Left Front Coy	J.S.S.
Do	18.6.18		A.Coy Support Coy, B Coy Reserve Coy.	J.P.N.
Do	19.6.18		Line Quiet nothing to report. Working parties supplied	J.Q.L.
Do	20.6.18		Do	J.Q.L.
Do	21.6.18		Inter Coy Relief. A Coy relieved C Coy in Right Front Subsector. B Coy relieved D Coy in Left Front Subsector.	J.Q.L.
Do	22.6.18		Line Quiet, nothing to report. Working parties supplied	J.Q.L.
Do	23.6.18		Do	J.Q.L.
Do	24.6.18		Do	J.Q.L.
Do	25.6.18		Battalion was relieved in Line by 4/5" Black Watch. A Coy by B Coy 4/5" Black Watch B Coy by C Coy 4/5 Black Watch. C Coy by A Coy 4/5 Black Watch. D Coy by D Coy 4/5 Black Watch. Battalion moved out billets at WAKEFIELD Camp. Capt. E.S.Fiddes joined for duty.	J.Q.L.
WAKEFIELD Camp	26.6.18		Battalion spent day cleaning up and reorganising. Baths A 915. Coy.	J.Q.L.
Do	27.6.18		Battalion Employed on Coy Training. A Coy at Rifle Range. C+D Coy at Baths	J.Q.L.
Do	28.6.18		Do arms instruction. B Coy at Rifle Range.	S.Q.L.
Do	29.6.18		Do Rifles inspected by Armourer Y/Sergeant. D Coy at Rifle Range	J.Q.L.
Do	30.6.18		Battalion Church Parade.	N.Q.L.
			Reinforcements 9 Officers and 276 O.R. Joined for duty. Casualties 2 O.R. Killed, 13 O.R. wounded.	J.Q.L.

John P. Murray Lt.Col.
Comd. 9/Bt (Hds) H. Royal Scots

CONFIDENTIAL

WAR DIARY

9TH BATTN. THE ROYAL SCOTS

JULY 1918

(6339) Wt. W160/M3016 1,500,000 10/17 McA & W Ltd (E 1898) Forms W3091. Army Form W.3091.

Cover for Documents.

Nature of Enclosures.

Notes, or Letters written.

WAR DIARY
or
INTELLIGENCE SUMMARY.
(Erase heading not required.)

Army Form C. 2118.

Place	Date	Hour	Summary of Events and Information	Remarks and references to Appendices
WAKEFIELD CAMP nr ARRAS	1-7-18	—	Coy training. Bath.	H.Q.S.
do	2-7-18	—	Coy training	H.Q.S.
do	3-7-18	—	Batt. relieved 6th Cameron Hrs with Rgt Sub sector Left Rd front on night of 3/4th. Rels C Coy Rgt front by D Coy, Left front by H Coy Support Coy by B Coy, Reserve Coy by B Coy Reserve. Batt HQ H.14.c.65.30.	H.Q.S.
LINE	4-7-18 8-7-18		Few very quiet. Nothing to report	H.Q.S.
do	9-7-18		Rgt. relieved by 7th K.O.S.B. on the Left Sector Rgt blns relieved on night of 9/10th as under: B Coy Reserve C Coy relieved by D Coy 7/K.O.S.B. D Coy relieved by A Coy 7/K.O.S.B. B Coy relieved by C Coy 7/K.O.S.B. A Coy relieved by B Coy 7/K.O.S.B. Dispositions of Battln Platoons. Batt HQ in Rly cutting at H.14.a.17.1. B Coy HQ in Rly cutting at H.14.a.1.9. 3 Platoon in Rly cutting 3 on L TILLOY TRENCH D Coy Coy HQ at H9.9.90 2 platoons in 1515 TRENCH between CAM AVE and KEFFIR TRENCH H14.a. A Coy Coy HQ H.9.d.25.30. 4 Platoons in Trench running through CAM AVENUE in H.9. C Coy Coy HQ of H14 b.6.c. One Platoon in Trench N of HOLLOW LANE in H.14.b. 3 Platoons in Trench S of HOLLOW LANE — H.14.b.	H.Q.S.
LINE	10-7-18 11-7-18		Line quiet. Nothing to report.	H.Q.S.
LINE	12-7-18		Batt. relieved in Reserve by 4th Bn Canadian Rgt Mtd Canadian Lf Bn and th. Offr. accompanies detail in Rel. Batt. to ARRAS arriving at 11.30 PM 13th Coys. were relieved by corresponding Coys of 1st Canadian Batt.	H.Q.S.
ARRAS	13-7-18		Batt. moved by road to Rly Railway to CAM BRIGNEUL arriving at G.H.Q. Reserve area this day 11.15 AM. Transferred by road (details Batt. at HAINES LES DUISANS moved by rail and rejoined Batt. at CAMPIGNEUL.	H.Q.S.
CAMPIGNEUL	14-7-18		Reorganizing Batt. Cleaning of Clothes & Equip.	H.Q.S.

John L. Officers
Lieut Colonel
Comdg 7th British th. Royal Regt

Reference Map 51 8 NW   Army Form C. 2118.

WAR DIARY
or
INTELLIGENCE SUMMARY.
(Erase heading not required.)

Instructions regarding War Diaries and Intelligence
Summaries are contained in F. S. Regs., Part II.
and the Staff Manual respectively. Title pages
will be prepared in manuscript.

Place	Date	Hour	Summary of Events and Information	Remarks and references to Appendices
CAMBLIGNEUL	15.7.18		Closing up and reorganising	H.Q.S.
do	16.7.18		Batt. moves to new area transferring from XVII Corps to 20th French Corps. Entraining station SAVY. Batt. marches to entraining station 8.1-30 A.M.	H.Q.S.
Rly Mt. BEAUVAIS Lea Mat N° 32			Entraining SAVY for PONT ST. MAXENCE arriving 12.40 A.M. 17th	H.Q.S.
MONCEAUX	17.7.18		Detrained at PONT ST MAXENCE and marched to MONCEAUX arriving there at 3-30 A.M. where Batt. was accommodated in Billets.	H.Q.S.
do	18.7.18		Rest. March. Batt. Inspection of Battn. by Corps. G. Commanding Officer.	H.Q.S.
do	19.7.18		Order received at 4.20 A.M. Batt. to be ready to move by 5 A.M. At 7.15 A.M. Batt. marches to TOURTEAU COURT where it bivouaced HAUT FONTAINE arriving there at 4.20 P.M. Batt. bivouaced in woods S. of village. Transport moves by road	H.Q.S.
HAUTE FONTAINE	20.7.18		Coy Inspection. Orders received at 4 P.M. to be ready to move, but subsequently cancelled. Very heavy rain. Bn accommodated in out houses of CHATEAU - shortage of space.	H.Q.S.
do	21.7.18		Batt. resting and completing Battle Equipment. Orders received to move by march route to FORET DOMINALE DE RETZ. starting at 10.20 P.M.	H.Q.S.
FORET DOMINALE DE RETZ	22.7.18		Batt. arrives at 3 A.M. and BIVOUACED in wood to md NORTH of M. in MON PRE DE MON GOBERT. Batt. moved off from bivouacs at 7 P.M. are proceeded by march route through CHAUDON CHAZELLE and retains the Rt. of CAPT BANFORD'S N Battn. 1st Div. U.S. Army and arrives in support of other 2 Battns of the Bde W & K.S.B. & 10th S.R. Rifles H.Q. at 2 in NORTH of Rd E. in CHAZELLE. B & D Coys move 12.40 A.C. by S of VISIGNEUX FARM. Rly. comps by 3.20 A.M.	H.Q.S.
LINE	23.7.18		Batt. relieves 1/5 K.S.B. in Regt Res Sector. B Coy Regt O. Fwd by A Coy Batt Coy, D Coy left front by C Coy Reserve Coy Z. HQ. 500 M of V in VISIGNEUX. Front line Ridcan N° 3 through B.J of BUSANCY	H.Q.P. H.Q.S.
do	24.7.18		Position Res'd. was hardly shelled throughout the day. Otherwise nothing to report	H.Q.S.
do	25.7.18		7th Batt. was relieved by 5th London the. Very heavy shelling during relief	H.Q.S.

John Milner Lieut Colonel
Comdg 7/L Royal Scots.

Army Form C. 2118.

WAR DIARY
or
INTELLIGENCE SUMMARY.
(Erase heading not required.)

Instructions regarding War Diaries and Intelligence Summaries are contained in F. S. Regs., Part II. and the Staff Manual respectively. Title pages will be prepared in manuscript.

Place	Date	Hour	Summary of Events and Information	Remarks and references to Appendices
LINE + CHAUDUN	26-7-18		Relief by 5" Londons Bn. completed by 1:15 AM. + Bn. moved back to Divn Reserve + took over POSTS E of CHAUDUN. B.H.Q. 500780. S.E of A in CHAUDUN. All Coys. were employed in digging a system of POSTS between PLOISY + CHAZELLE which was 6 be manned ; also as Divnl Reserve in case of enemy attack.	J.B.M.
do	27-7-18		Batt. carried out digging as on 26 th. Weather very bad.	J.B.M.
do	28-7-18		Batt. received orders at 6.20 P.M. to relieve the 6/ French 2nd Regt. west of 5 6 "French 2/" Regt in Line SOUTH of VILLEMONTOIRE. Batt. moved at 11.15 P.M.	J.B.M.
LINE	29-7-18		Relief completed by 3.30 A.M. A C + D Coys in front line B Coy in reserve. 7/8" K.O.S.B. on left flank, 54 French 2/Regt. on right flank. Batt. H.Q. at RAPERIE.	J.B.M.
LINE	30-7-18		Batt. H.Q. moved back to TRENCH SOUTH of R in CHARINTINY. B Coy HQ. + 2 Platoons took over A.Q. at RAPERIE.	J.B.M.
LINE	31-7-18		Batt. remained as on 30 st. Orders received for attack in wooded hillocks to be carried out on 1-8-18	J.B.M.
			Casualties for the month :- Officers 2 killed, 4 wounded, 1 wounded at duty. O/Rs 20 killed, 144 wounded, 6 wounded at duty, 6 missing.	
			Reinforcements for the month 1 Capt G. Borthwick and 135 O.R.	
			Weather during the month very changeable.	
			The General health of the Battalion was good.	

John B Muir Lieut Colonel
Comdg 9" Bn (Hrs) The Royal Scots

SECRET   Copy No. 11

OPERATION ORDER No. 14

Ref Map 51° NW. 1/20,000

RELIEF	1.	The Battn will relieve the 6th Cameron Hrs in the the Right Subsector, Left Bde front, on night 3/4th July 1918.
DISPOSITION	2.	C Coy Right Front Coy D Coy Left Front Coy A Coy Support Coy B Reserve " Battn HQ H.10.c.65.30.
STARTING TIME	3.	9-15 P.M.
STARTING POINT	4.	NORTH end of camp
ORDER of MARCH	5.	C. D. Bn HQ A. B. Coys will move by platoons at 100 yards interval
ROUTE	6.	Track 'A' - Plank Road
GUIDES	7.	Guides, 1 per coy HQ and 1 per platoon will meet coys at junction of EFFIE TRENCH and GAVRELLE
STORES	8.	All signalling and mess stores will be stacked at Orderly Room by 9 P.M.
LEWIS GUNS	9.	Lewis Guns and ammunition will be stacked at Orderly Room by 9 P.M. One man per coy, will accompany the limber and will be responsible for destribution at the other end.
TRENCH STORES	10.	All Trench Stores, defence schemes, aeroplane photos, maps tools, explosives etc. will be taken over and receipts given A consolidated list will be sent to Bn HQ by 4 P.M. on 4th Inst.
GENERAL	11.	Coy. Commanders will report personally to Commanding Officer that Huts and ground in vicinity of Huts has been left clean one hour before moving off.
COMPLETION of RELIEF	12.	Completion of relief will be wired to Battn HQ useing code word "CAT"

ACKNOWLEDGE

2-7-18   9th Bn (Hrs) The Royal Scots

                                                    Capt a/adjt

Copy No. 1. OC A Coy
   "   2.   " B "
   "   3.   " C "
   "   4.   " D "
   "   5. OC 6 Cameron Hrs
   "   6. Spec. Officer
   "   7. T.O.
   "   8. QM
   "   9. Adjt
   "   10. File
   "   11. War Diary

SECRET   COPY No. 8

OPERATION ORDER No. 15

Ref. Map 51ᴮ NW 1/20,000

RELIEF	1	The Battn will be relieved by 7/8ᵗʰ K.O.S.B. in the right subsector Left Section on night of 9/10ᵗʰ inst and will go into Bde Reserve. C Coy relieved by D Coy K.O.S.B. B Coy relieved by C Coy K.O.S.B. D " " A " A " " B
GUIDES	2	Coys will supply guides 1 pr platoon and 1 pr Coy H.Q. rendezvous and times as under. C Coy Junction CASTLE LANE and CAMERON TRENCH at 10·30 P.M. Guides will take 13 & 14 Platoons 7/8ᵗʰ KOSB up LEMON TRENCH and 15 & 16 Platoons KOSB up CAMEL AVENUE D Coy Junction EFFIE TRENCH & CASTLE LANE at 10·40 P.M. B Coy Junction EFFIE SWITCH & CAMERON TRENCH at 10·30 P.M. A Coy. No guides required. Advance party 7/8ᵗʰ KOSB will act as guides
DISPOSITIONS IN RESERVE	3	Battn H.Q. will be in Rly cutting at H.14.a.1.7. B Coy. Coy H.Q. in cutting at H.14.a.1.9. 3 platoons in cutting and one in TILLOY TRENCH in H.14.a. D Coy. Coy H.Q. at H.9.a.9.0. 4 Platoons in ISIS TRENCH between CAM AVE and EFFIE TRENCH A Coy. Coy H.Q. H.9.c.25.20 4 Platoons in trench near junction running N & S. through CAM AVE in H.9.c. C Coy. Coy H.Q. at H.14.b.6.5. 1 Platoon in trench N. of HOLLINS LANE in H.14.b. 3 platoons in trench S of HOLLINS LANE in H.14.b. Advance parties already detailed will act as guides to their coys. after relief.
TRENCH STORES	4	All trench stores, maps, work on hand, defence schemes, SOS Grenades, explosives etc will be handed over and receipts obtained A consolidated list will be sent to Bn H.Q. by 2 P.M. 10ᵗʰ inst.
STORES	5	Mess Stores, Lewis Guns & Ammunition etc will be moved by Coy arrangements.
GENERAL	6	All trenches, dugouts, shelters, Latrines, cookhouses etc will be left scrupulously clean
COMPLETION of RELIEF	7	Completion of relief will be wired to Bn H.Q. using code word "WORK". Occupation of reserve positions will be reported to Bn H.Q. by runner.

ACKNOWLEDGE

8-7-18   Capt & Adjt
                                                   9ᵗʰ Royal Scots

DISTRIBUTION
Copy No. 1 to O.C. A Coy
"   " 2 "   B
"   " 3 "   C
"   " 4 "   D
"   " 5 " 7/8ᵗʰ KOSB
"   " 6 "   Adjt
"   " 7 "   7 de
"   " 8 "   War Diary

SECRET   COPY No 9

OPERATION ORDER No 16

Ref Map 51B. 1/20,000

RELIEF	1	The Battn will be relieved in Brigade Reserve by the 4th Canadian Battn on night of 12/13th Inst and will proceed to billets in ARRAS. A Coy will be relieved by A Coy 4th Bn Canadian B " " " " B " " " C " " " " C " " " D " " " " D " " "
GUIDES	2	Coys will supply guides 1 per platoon and 1 for Coy H.Q. to be at Battn HQ at 7-30 P.M.
ORDER OF RELIEF	3	Battn H.Q, B, A, C, D Coys Coys will move by platoons at 100 yds interval
ROUTE	4	Bn HQ & B by GAVRELLE Road to fork roads in H.13.b. A & C Coy by HOLLINS LANE – TILLOY TRENCH to H.14.a.b.2. thence main road to fork roads in H.13.b. D Coy EFFIE TRENCH – GAVRELLE ROAD to fork roads in H.13.b. Bn HQ & all Coys thence by main road through BLANGY – ST NICHOLAS to Seven Roads Square where Coys will meet advance party who will guide them to their respective billets.
STORES	5	Mess Stores, camp kettles and all surplus stores will be sent to Bn HQ by 9-30 PM.
LEWIS GUNS	6	All Lewis Guns & Ammunition will be carried.
TRENCH STORES	7	All Trench Stores, maps, air photos, work on hand, S.O.S grenades, explosives etc will be handed over and receipt obtained, which will be sent to Bn HQ immediately on arrival in billets. Attention is drawn to para 2 of Administrative Instructions.
DUTY	8	The following Officers & N.C.Os. will be left with the relieving unit until 10 A.M. on day after relief, they will thereafter rejoin the Bn in ARRAS :- Battn HQ Lieut F.M. Ross and each Coy 1 officer for Coy H.Q. and 1 N.C.O per platoon HQ
GENERAL	9	All trenches, dugouts, shelters, cookhouses latrines etc will be left scrupulously clean
COMPLETION OF RELIEF	10	Completion of relief will be reported to Bn HQ by wire or runner using code word "SIGNALS" OC Coys will report personally that Coys are complete in billets

Ron Whytock Lieut and Adjt
9th Royal Scots

11-7-18
Issued at 9 PM
DISTRIBUTION
Copy No 1 OC A Coy
2 " B "
3 " C "
4 " D "
5 Spec Officer
6 QM & TO
7 Adjutant
8 File
9 War Diary

SECRET

Administrative Instructions issued with Operation Order No. 9

1. BILLETS

On relief, the Battalion will be accommodated in ARRAS as follows:-

46 RUE DES TROIS VERGES		BATTN. H.Q
44 RUE DES TROIS VISAGES		
10,12 RUE ERNEST DE LAUNOY	}	OFFICERS
9 RUE DE LA CAISSE D'EPARGNE		
HOTEL DE VILLE	} CELLARS	OTHER RANKS
(15?) PLACE		

2. BILLETING PARTIES

O.C. Companies will detail Billeting parties of 1 NCO per platoon and 1 NCO for Coy H.Q. to report to Lieut A.J. Hughson at Bn.H.Q. at 8.30 a.m. on 12th inst. The party will thereafter report to Town Commandant, ARRAS; PLACE ADOLPHE LENALET, Corner of RUE DES RAYES COCHEZES at 10 am 12th inst. Billet Locations will be waiting to show Billeting Officer his Billeting area.

3. ARRAS TOWN ORDERS

Town orders will be strictly enforced. The Town Commandant will be notified when Billets are vacated.
Troops are not allowed outside their billeting area. They will keep under cover during the hours of daylight and special precautions will be taken to ensure that no unusual movement is observable from the air. All shots are out of bounds to S.O.S. Troops will not be allowed to congregate in the PLACES. O.C. Coys will post Aeroplane Sentries and Gas Guards.

4. HANDING OVER

Great care will be exercised in handing over all French Stores. Receipts will be carefully checked with what is actually handed over before sending into Bde.H.Q. This will avoid correspondence later. Receipts will be submitted to Bn A.Q in triplicate.

5. RATIONS

Consequent upon troops having two days rations, Rations will not be brought to the line on night 11th inst.

6. COOKERS Cookers will be brought into Arras but not before 9 pm on 12th inst. They will then be sheltered from view among Buildings.

7. TRANSPORT The Quartermaster will arrange direct with O.C. No.4 Coy train for any transport he may require to convey kits etc. into ARRAS.

8. FUTURE ARRANGEMENTS

Battalion will probably move to CAUCOURT AREA on 13th inst. O.C. Coys will detail Billeting Party to be held in readiness to move at short notice by motor lorry on 12th inst or early on 13th inst to take over Billets in new area. Lieut L.S. Gould will take command. Cpl Fitzsimmons for Bn. H.Q. 1 NCO per platoon and 1 for Coy H.Q. Transport Officer and Quartermaster will be prepared to hand over Transport lines and Coy. Stores to unit of 1st Canadian Inf. Bde. Further orders will be issued on arrival of 1st Canadian Inf. Bde.

11-7-18.

Lt. Whitlock Lieut
Adjt.

SECRET   COPY No. 9

OPERATION ORDER No. 17

Ref Map 51c NE 1/20,000

MOVE.	1.	The Batt. will move by road & light railway to billets in CAMBLIGNEUL on 13th inst. and will be in G.H.Q. Reserve. Entraining Station ANZIN detraining station VILLERS CHATEL
STARTING TIME	2.	1-30 P.M.
STARTING POINT	3.	Street in front of Batt. H.Q.
ORDER OF MARCH	4.	Batt. H.Q. D.A.C.B. Coys. The Batt. will move by Coys at 100 yds interval before entraining and after detraining.
ROUTE	5.	By "Seven Roads Square" to ST CATHERINE thence to ANZIN
ENTRAINING	6.	On arrival at ANZIN the Batt. will form up as follows :- Batt. H.Q. D.A. & C Coys in open space at L.6.c.11. B Coy in open space at G.7 & G.7. Each Coy will detail one officer to report to the Adjt. at L.6.c.11. when he will be allotted train accommodation and given instructions re entraining. The officer detailed for this duty will hand entraining strength of his Coy to the adjutant. O.C. Coys will reconnoitre all routes and approaches to station on morning of 13th Inst.
STORES	7.	Mess Stores etc will be stacked at Batt. H.Q. by 1 P.M. on 13th Inst.
LEWIS GUNS	8.	Lewis Guns and Ammunition will be carried.
GENERAL	9.	Advance parties will meet Coys at detraining Station and guide Coys to billets. All billets in ARRAS will be left in a clean and sanitary condition. O.C. Coys will report one hour before moving off that this has been done. During the move strict march & train discipline will be enforced. Men will NOT be allowed to ride with legs hanging outside trucks or in any other way that seems dangerous to the O.C. truck O.C. Coys will report arrival in Billets to Batt. O. Room

ACKNOWLEDGE

Ron Whytock
Lieut and Adjt
9th Royal Scots

12-7-18

DISTRIBUTION
Copy No. 1   O.C. A Coy
"   2   " B "
"   3   " C "
"   4   " D "
"   5   Spec. Officer
"   6   T.O. & Q.M.
"   7   Adjt
"   8   File
"   9   War Diary

SECRET   COPY N° 10

OPERATION ORDER N° 173

Ref. Map (Spec sheet attached) 51ᴱ 1/40,000

MOVE	1	The Batt. less A Coy and cooker will move to new area. entraining at SAVY at 5.26 AM on 16th Inst. Transport less A Coy cooker will entrain at 3.26 AM at SAVY Stn moving off at 12.30 AM. A Coy and cookers will move off at 11.45 AM to be at SAVY Stn at 2.26 AM. and will report to RTO or Staff Captain and will detail 2 officers and 100 ORs to unload the first four trains at detraining station.
STARTING TIME	2	The Batt. less A Coy & transport - 1-45 AM
STARTING POINT	3	Road Junction opposite Batt. H.Q.
ROUTE	4	Road through W.14 d & c — W.13 central — VILLERS CHATEL — Cross Roads V.18.d.20 — MINGOVAL — Souther Road to V.23.c.6.9. — Cross Roads V.29.a.6.4. — road junction V.29.c.4.9 — road junction D.5.b.20 — Level crossing D.5.a.88 — Station. Batt. Scouts will act as guides at all road crossings
ORDER OF MARCH	5	Batt HQ B.D.C. 100 yards between Coys
LEWIS GUNS	6	Lewis Guns and ammunition will be carried to SAVY STN. on transport and will be drawn there and will remain in possession of L.G. Sections
STORES	7	Officers Valises. Mess stores etc. will be stacked at QM stores by 12 midnight. A Coy's at once.
ENTRAINING	8	Entraining Officer (Lt RM WHYTOCK) will report to Capt POWER at 4.15 AM. at SAVY STN. with full entraining strength including transport. by Coys. 2/Lt Banks and 1 NCO per Coy and 1 for Bn HQ will report to Staff Capt at 2.26 AM and will act as billeting party. They will report to 2/Lt Banks at Bn H.Q at 11-30 PM On arrival at station each Coy will send one officer to report to Lieut WHYTOCK to be shown train accommodation
GENERAL	9	Coy commanders have will report to him at 11-30 AM. Major Lindsay, Adjt. M.O. & O.C. B.C. & Coy horses will report to Coy O & Batt. H.Q. respectively at 1-30 A.M. Billets will be left scrupulously clear. All water bottles will be filled before moving off ACKNOWLEDGE.

15·7·18   C.H.S./adj
                                              9 Royal Scots.

DISTRIBUTION
Copy N° 1   Lt Whytock
    " 2   2/Lt Banks
    " 3   OC A Coy
    " 4   B   "
    " 5   C   "
    " 6   D   "
    " 7   Spec. Officers
    " 8   Adjt
    " 9   File
    " 10 War Diary

SECRET   Copy No 9

OPERATION ORDER No 18

Ref Map SOISSONS Sheet no 33

MOVE	1	The Battn will relieve troops of 1st American Bde commanded by Major HUNT and will be accommodated about VISIGNEUX FARM
DISPOSITIONS	2	Right Front 9/8'KOSB. Left Front 10th Scottish Rifles 1/9th Royal Scots in Support Battn H.Q. at CHAZELLE A & C Coys front support. D Coy Close support, B Coy Reserve.
STARTING TIME	3	7 P.M.
" POINT	4	Road junction WEST END of wood
ROUTE	5	VILLERS COTERET - SOISSONS Road to CRAVANÇON FARM - CHAUDON. 100 yards between platoons. 300 yds between Battalions
GUIDES	6	Guides will be met on road midway between CHAUDON and CRAVANÇON FARM at 9.10 P.M.
ORDER OF MARCH	7	A C D B Coys Battn H.Q.
LEWIS GUNS	8	Lewis Guns and Ammunition will be packed on transport at Bn HQ at 6.15 PM and will be drawn at new Bn HQ VISIGNEUX FARM
WATER TINS	9	Water tins will also be drawn as above no of tins per coy as already stated
MESS STORES	10	Mess stores for the line will be handed over to T.O. at 6 PM and will be drawn at new Bn HQ.
COMPLETION OF RELIEF	11	Completion of relief will be reported as soon as possible to Bn H.Q.
ECHELON B	12	Transport, Echelon B & details will stand fast pending further orders

22.7.18   Capt & Adjt
                                                   9th Royal Scots

DISTRIBUTION
Copy no 1   OC A Coy
       2   " B "
       3   " C "
       4   " D "
       5   Spec Officers
       6   QM   TO
       7   Adjt
       8   File
       9   War Diary

SECRET

ADMINISTRATIVE INSTRUCTIONS No 2

MOVE   1.   The Battn will move to billets in CAMBLIGNEUL on 13th Inst. Further instructions.

BILLETING PARTY   2.   O.C. Coy will detail 1 senior N.C.O. to report to Staff Captain at RONZ POINT ARRAS at 9.45 AM. on 12th Inst. This N.C.O. will travel by motor lorry to CAMBLIGNEUL and take over transport lines allotted to the Battn. He will remain there overnight 12/13th and will meet Battn transport on arrival about 12 noon 13th. Rations for 12th will be carried.
Lieut W.S. LESLIE and Cpl Fitzsimmons and one N.C.O. per Coy (not as stated in Administrative Instruction No 1 para 8 dated 10.7.18) will report to Staff Captain at 6.10 AM on 13th Inst at ARTILLERY CORNER L.12.a.4.8. They will proceed by train leaving ARTILLERY CORNER at 6.20 AM. The above officer will be in possession of LENS map 1/100.000 and a piece of chalk.

TRANSPORT   3.   Para 7 of Administrative Instruction No 1 is hereby cancelled.
One lorry is placed at the disposal of the Battn, which you will report in the first instance to a representative to be detailed by the Transport Officer at cross Roads K.12.c.3.4. AGNES-LES-DUISANS at 8AM on 13th Inst. This lorry will afterwards report to the Quartermaster, who will take all his stores from AGNES LES DUISANS to CAMBLIGNEUL.

TRANSPORT LINES   4.   The Bde Transport Officer will inspect transport lines before leaving AGNES-LES-DUISANS.
Tents, Tarpaulins &c, not the property of the unit will be handed over to the Town Commandant and receipts obtained and forwarded to Bn HQ.

RAILHEAD & REFILLING   5.   HQ 15th Divisional Train moves to FREVIN CAPELLE which becomes the Railhead. Arrangements for refilling will be wired direct to Q.M.

BATHS   6.   Baths are CAUCOURT. Allotment will be published shortly.

DRAFTS & DETACHMENTS   7.   All drafts and details at present in AGNES-LES-DUISANS will report to Battn at CAMBLIGNEUL.
N.C.Os & men at present attached to 185 Tunnelling Coy will report to their respective Coys in ARRAS.

Ron Whytock Capt/adjt
9 Royal Scots

11-7-18

Confidential

98 41

War Diary

9th Battn (H.) The Royal Scots

From 1.8.18
To 31.8.18

39 R.

Ref. Maps OUCHY 1/20.000
Special Sheet BEUVRY 32. 57C/40.000
LENS II 1/100.000 57/5.N.W. 1/20.000
  H3 1/40.000
  G4 1/100.000
  44 M.N.W 3 1/10.000

Army Form C. 2118.

WAR DIARY or INTELLIGENCE SUMMARY.
(Erase heading not required.)

9th Batt (Tpr) The Royal Scots

Place	Date	Hour	Summary of Events and Information	Remarks and references to Appendices
Line	1-8-18		Under cover of darkness Battalion moved into assembly positions as follows. D.Coy. also on 28-7-18.	
			C.Coy and 3 Platoons of B.Coy were dug in close behind. Remaining platoon of B.Coy was detailed as	
			Liaison platoon between right of D.Coy and Left of 12th French Division who were to attack in conjunction.	
			A.Coy. was dug in behind C + B.Coys Objectives as shown on map. Battn H.Q. occupied H.Q. in RAPERIE	
			10th Scottish Rifles who were to advance through the Battn were assembled behind till 8.30 am Battn	
			H.Q. were notified that Zero hour would be 9 a.m. Artillery Barrage started at 9.2 am at 9.3 a.m.	
			First wave of D.Coy advanced and met heavy enemy M.G. fire, assembled- J.D Coy following in artillery	
			formation climbing gun for moment from right flank. 12th French Div. on our right was held up by	
			machine gun fire. A Very enemy barrage came down about 350 yds behind our front line.	
			At 9.7 am C.Coy. followed D.Coy and attained about 250 y.ds before being held up by Machine Gunfire	
			At 10.5 am word was received at H.Q. that C.Coy. was unable to advance any further owing to	
			strong enemy opposition. At this time enemy kept up continual sniping on our wounded who were	
			attempting to leave the field. At 12 noon 4/5th Black Watch on left and 5th Gordons on right came up	
			to within 800 yds of our position in artillery formation, when they extended and ultimately reinforced	
			the jumping off line. At 1.30 p.m. The enemy counter attacked the Left flank of the 12th French Div. and	
			captured a few prisoners. At 2/4 pm orders were received that A.Coy 9th Royal 1 Scots and 10th Scottish Rifles	

W.L Mumby Major

WAR DIARY / INTELLIGENCE SUMMARY

Army Form C. 2118.

Lib Chaps - OULCHY 1/20,000
Special Sheet BEAUVAIS 32. 51c 1/40,000
LENS 11 1/100,000 51n N.W. 1/20,000
44 B 1/20,000
44 A 1/40,000
44 N N.W. 3 1/10,000

9th Bn (W) Bl.W. 1 Scot.

Place	Date	Hour	Summary of Events and Information	Remarks and references to Appendices
			10cc to continue the attack. Zero hour being 3.30 p.m. Bttn at 2.20 p.m. Enemy was found digging in. Machine Guns on our front. This was reported to Bde. A Coy advanced and was immediately held up by heavy M.G. fire but managed to get 100 yds from jumping off position before being finally held up. The French on our right who were to attack in conjunction with A Coy were not able to leave their assembly position owing to heavy enemy fire. 10th Scottish Rifles were unable to advance "A" Coy being unable to get forward. The enemy kept a barrage M.G. fire on our front till darkness fell when A Bttn was relieved by 4/5th Black Watch and withdrew to Railway Tunnel 1/2 miles due South of last E in LECHELLE. On information being received that enemy had withdrawn from his position Several patrols were organised at 4 p.m. also was received that Battalion front was at 6 p.m. and take up position formerly held before the attack. B.H.Q. at RAPERIE. at 11p.m. orders were received that 2 Coys were to proceed and dig positions on high ground N of TAUX.	G.R.S. G.R.S.
Live	2.8.18			
Live	3.8.18		At 5 a.m. orders were issued that Battalion would embus at VERZY at 10 a.m. On arrival thus at new ground West knows were not available and Battalion proceeded by march route to Soucy Stopping at Transport lines at MONTGOBERT WOOD for dinner. Battn then billets & marched by PUISEUX & SOUCY that Battn. went into billets and remained the night.	G.R.S. G.R.S.
SOUCY MONCEAUX	4.8.18		Battn entrained at SOUCY for MONCEAUX arriving there at 9.30 p.m. when billets were occupied.	

W.F.Hinshaw Major

Army Form C. 2118.

WAR DIARY
or
INTELLIGENCE SUMMARY.
(Erase heading not required.)

9th Bedr (Ryr) The Royal Scots

Place	Date	Hour	Summary of Events and Information	Remarks and references to Appendices
MONCEAUX	5.8.18		Battalion remained at Monceaux and has engaged cleaning up and bathing.	Q.S.
Do	6.8.18		Battalion entrained at PONT ST MAXENCE starting at 11 a.m. and moved to PETIT HOUVIN	Q.S.
MAIZIERES	7.8.18		Were Battalion detrained and marched to MAIZIERES were billeted, move completed by 4.30 pm	Q.S.
"	8.8.18		Battalion remained in billets and Coys re-organised and recels app Battle drivers in lieu of Battalion resonwise inspected by Commanding Officer	Q.S.
"	9.8.18		Battalion spent day in bathing and in coys inspected by Commanding Officer.	Q.S.
"	10.8.18		Battalion engaged in Coy Training, Recreational Games in afternoon	Q.S.
"	11.8.18		Rehearsal Ceremonial Parade. Presentation of French decorations, also Church Parade.	Q.S.
"	12.8.18		Ceremonial Parade. Presentation of French Decorations by Divisional Commander 15 Division at (H4b44) Sheet 51C 1/40.000) at 10 a.m. The following was decorated:- Legion of Honour (Chevalier) Lt Col J.S. MUIR D.S.O. Medaille Militaire 357055 Sgt J. FRASER Croix de Guerre (Palms) Lt J.S. THOMSON M.C. 350314 Cpl P/Sgt K.M. BAIRD Lt A.J. HUGHSON 352321 Pte W. DOBBIN M.M. Croix de Guerre (Stone) 351191 9/Sgt A. LOCKIE 350979 Pte W. BLYTHE 42525 Pte E.J. McWHIRTER 202667 - A. COPE 352338 - W. PENNING	Q.S.

W.J. Winterbury Maj

WAR DIARY
INTELLIGENCE SUMMARY

(Erase heading not required.)

Army Form C. 2118.

9th Batt. (H.P.) The Royal Scots

Place	Date	Hour	Summary of Events and Information	Remarks and references to Appendices
MAIZIÈRES	13.8.18		After the Presentation, the Divisional Commander, in his speech commented on the great and gallant work done by the Battalion. Battalion engaged in Coy Training. Recreational games in afternoon.	Q.S.
D°	14.8.18		D°. Battalion Sports from 2 p.m. Divisional Band was in attendance.	Q.S.
D°	15.8.18		Battalion engaged in Coy Training.	Q.S.
D°	16.8.18		Battalion assigned fatigues for men on following day.	Q.S.
D°	17.8.18		Battalion moved by Bus to ARRAS to join Corps Reserve and relieved 1/2" London Regt. Starting bus 6 p.m. Starting point G.23.c.75.00	Q.S.
ARRAS	18.8.18		C.D. Coys carried on Coy Training. A & B Coys were ordered to move into the line (ARRAS SECTOR) and take the place of two Coys 10 Scottish Rifles who were pushing forward in fighting patrol formation to try and establish touch with the enemy. A Coy was under the direct orders of O.C. 10th Scottish Rifles and was in Tilloy Reserve System. B Coy was in Tilloy Support System and Came under the orders of O.C. 7/8 K.O.S.B. About 9 p.m. a 19th B Coy came under the orders of O.C. 10th Scottish Rifles and the following orders were issued. B Coy 10 Scottish Rifles will push forward into No Mans Land as at patrolbush in chain of posts from the CAMBRAI ROAD to the English B.M. who had attained in the left front just south of the STUMPS. Having done this they were to push out a couple of Strong patrols with a view to discovering whether the enemy held his first two systems of trenches. If these trenches were unoccupied A & B Coys of	

W.B. Wintringham Maj

WAR DIARY
INTELLIGENCE SUMMARY

9th Batt (T.F.) Vth Royal Scots

Army Form C. 2118.

Place	Date	Hour	Summary of Events and Information	Remarks and references to Appendices
ARRAS	19.8.18		9 Royal Scots were to push forward and occupy them in preparation of the 6th Bgde moved forward to immediately behind the front line and awaited their forward positions all night the Bgde were ordered about 7am on morning of 20" to return to their former positions in the protest had defeated the enemy to to holding his front line. About 10am on morning of 21" A.P.H Bgde B 9 Royal Scots were relieved and rejoined The Battalion in ARRAS about 2am	A.Q.S
	20.8.18		C & B. Cys. Carried out Coy Training, musketry, baths &c	A.Q.S
	21.8.18		Do	A.Q.S
	22.8.18		Battalion engaged in Coy Training Do	A.Q.S
	23.8.18		Do A.P.B Bgde rejoined Battalion who took over from 6 7th Bgde	A.Q.S
	24.8.18		Battalion entrained at ANZIN (distilling Gine) 2.12.2.a.4.8. at 5:55 am. and detained at CHATEAU de la HAIE, thence by march route to fields at MAROEUILLERS HUTS. R.26.2.8.7.	A.Q.S
MAROEUIL'S HUTS	25.8.18		Battalion formed by march route to MAIZINGARBE and occupied billets vacated by 13 Royal Scots.	A.Q.S
MAIZINGARBE	26.8.18		Battalion engaged making preparations of going into the line.	A.Q.S
"	27.8.18		Battalion relieved 9" Battalion Royal Sussex Regt in the line on night of 27/28" D Coy LEFT FRONT Coy. HQ at 6.30 & 9.4.	

W.C. Mornington Major

WAR DIARY
INTELLIGENCE SUMMARY
(Erase heading not required.)

Army Form C. 2118.

9 Batt (74) The Royal Scots

Place	Date	Hour	Summary of Events and Information	Remarks and references to Appendices
			C Coy Close Support Coy HQ at G.36.a.8.9. B.Coy Support Coy H.Q at G.29.c.5.3	
			A Coy Reserve Coy HQ at C.29.a.4.7. Batt HQ. at G.28.b.2.3.	
LINE	28.8.18		Line Quiet. Nothing to report.	A.25
D°	29.8.18		D°	A.25
D°	30.8.18		D° Lt Col J.B. Cluris D.S.O. ceased to command the Battalion on proceeding to U.K. 2nd Col J.A. Stephenson D.S.O. M.C. assumed command of the Battalion.	A.25
D°	31.8.18		D°	A.25
			Casualties for month Killed 5 O.R. 81 OR	
			Wounded 1 Off. 148 OR	
			Missing 10 OR	
			Strength of unit during month 13 Off 292 OR	
			Training staff 8 16 R.S. absorbed. 8 83 26 R°	
			The following decorations have been awarded 10 Military Medals	
			to pieces during the month have now got out the Matter of The R. Scots 8d	A.25

M. Munday Major

Confidential. 46/7s
—VB 42

40 R.l.

War Diary.
9th Battn (A&40) The Royal Scots

From 1-9-18. To 30-9-18.

Army Form C. 2118.

WAR DIARY
or
INTELLIGENCE SUMMARY.
(Erase heading not required.)

9th Battalion (Spr) The Royal Scots

Place	Date	Hour	Summary of Events and Information	Remarks and references to Appendices
Loos	1-9-18		Line quiet. Patrols sent out to locate enemy posts.	Nil
"	2-9-18		Line quiet. Bn. dispositions assigned shown as follows: 27 & 9 47.3 - G 23 c 9.0 and thence along H.25.a.6.1. Platoon O.C Coy in HEATH TRENCH (H.25.a.6.1). D Company relieved platoon of 9/13 K.O.S.B. in H.25.a.6.1. Platoon O.C. Coy in HEATH TRENCH (H.25.a.6.1). Changed places with platoon of A Coy occupying CHALK PIT ALLEY (G.30.d.9.5.75). Three troops were composed of four. There were no front-line troops per A Coy. B.Coy took over one company front up to the Black Match. 'C' Coy relieved by 10th S.R. and B Coy in support. Sub-sec troops holding positions: 1 Platoon Village Post G.29.c.5.3. 1 Platoon BELL POST G.29.a.6.4. 1 Platoon VILLAGE LANE G.28.b.7.3. 1 Platoon PASSAGE POST G.29.a.2.2. Above relieved by 10th S.R. and on relief occupied positions vacated by B Coy as follows: 1 Platoon TREBLE POST G.29.c.5.3. 1 Platoon AEROPLANE SOUTH POST G.29.a.4.0. 1 Platoon AEROPLANE NORTH POST B.29.c.1.7. 1 Platoon TRIANGLE POST G.29.c.4.3.	Nil
			After relief dispositions were as follows: Bn. HQ G.28.b.1.3. A Coy G.30.b.3.5.4.0. C/B Coy G.30.b.3.8. C Coy G.28.b.6.1. D Coy G.29.a.4.5.35.	
"	3-9-18		Line quiet. Patrols sent from A.B. to ascertain line of enemy camps in his front line. Strong patrols met empty. Enemy feeling very alert on Battalion front.	Nil
"	4-9-18		Line quiet.	Nil
"	5-9-18		Line quiet.	Nil
"	6-9-18		Line quiet.	Nil
"	7-9-18		Line quiet.	Nil
"	8-9-18		Battalion relieved in the line by 11/K.O.S.B. and thereafter moved to Billets in MAZINGARBE. Bn. in Divisional Reserve.	Nil
MAZINGARBE	9-9-18		Men employed cleaning equipt. and resting in Baths.	Nil
"	10-9-18		Company training. Baths and C.O inspection.	Nil
"	11-9-18		Company Training.	Nil
"	12-9-18		Company Training.	Nil
"	13-9-18		Baths.	Nil
"	14-9-18		Baths. A & B Coy relieved the two forward companies in trenches in G.24 and D. Bn. & Coy relieved the right B/5 Coy on the Left. Arrangements for relief made by Capt T.N. Somerville and 2nd Lieut J.H. Johnston. 'C' Coy relieves 'D' Coy S.R. in close support. 'D' Coy reliefs 'C' Coy in support line. Bn. HQ B.25 and 29.a.9.95. C Coy G.30.a.7.5.9.5. D Coy G.24.c.10.75.	Nil
Line	15-9-18		H.Q. A and B attacked at G.24.c.6.10.75. Patrol located enemy front line.	Nil

W. Chalmers Major
Cmdg 1/9th Bn R Scots

WAR DIARY or INTELLIGENCE SUMMARY

Army Form C. 2118.

9th Battn (Sclsr) The Royal Scots

(Erase heading not required.)

Place	Date	Hour	Summary of Events and Information	Remarks and references to Appendices
Loos	16.9.18		Line quiet. Patrolling enemy frontline	App
"	17.9.18		Line quiet. Patrolling enemy frontline	App
"	18.9.18		Line quiet. Nothing to report	App
"	19.9.18		Line quiet. Patrolling enemy frontline	App
"	20.9.18		Battalion relieved in the line at night 20/21st. C. Coy relieved by 13th by 1st Cogs A by D. Coy 9th by 13th A. 134th R.S. D. Coy 134th R.S. B. 13th in VERMELLES TUNNEL	App
VERMELLES	21.9.18		After raid Bn. moved to Battery Square &c.	App
"	22.9.18		Bn. relieved 9th Btn. Black Watch. 16th Division and 6th Scottish Rifles as follows:- A. Coy relieves B. Coy Scottish Rifles B. Coy relieves D. Coy 9th Black Watch C. Coy relieves B. Coy 9th Black Watch. D. Coy less one Platoon relieves C. Coy Scottish Rifles. 1 Platoon D. Coy relieves C. Coy 9th R.S. Cockcroft. Headquarters as before:- HQ G.11.c.3.3; A. Coy G.15.d.5.70. B. Coy G.4 & 9.5.0.5. C. Coy A.29.c.15.45. D. Coy G.11.+.7	App App
Loos	23.9.18		Line quiet. Active patrolling. Line front formed up G.11.3.3 on Trench 150 yds. from original front	App
"	24.9.18		Line quiet. Active patrolling	App
"	25.9.18		Line quiet. Active patrolling	App
"	26.9.18		Line quiet.	App
"	27.9.18		Line quiet. Active patrolling. Bn HQ B. Coy by 9th Scottish Rifles A and D Coys. Battalion relieved in line by A and C Coys 7th R.S. B. and one Coy 4th R.S. 6 Billets in VERMELLES TUNNEL	App
"	28.9.18		relieved by 7th R.S. Bn and one Coy 4th R.S. B at G 9 a 40. Bn in billets in VERMELLES Battn HQ A.7.c.cy and Batt HQ Cleaning up.	App
VERMELLES	29.9.18		Company training. Kit platoon inspection for Battn HQ and H & C Coys	App
"	30.9.18		Drafts came during month 4 Offrs — O.R 354 Casualties during month Killed — Officers — O.R. Wounded 5 Offrs 45 O.R. Missing 1 Officer and one other and the strength of the Battalion was excellent	App

Weather during month wholly good

[signature] Major
Comdg 9th Bn (Scs) Royal Scots

Army Form C. 2118.

WAR DIARY
or
INTELLIGENCE SUMMARY.
(Erase heading not required.)

Instructions regarding War Diaries and Intelligence Summaries are contained in F. S. Regs., Part II. and the Staff Manual respectively. Title pages will be prepared in manuscript.

Place	Date	Hour	Summary of Events and Information	Remarks and references to Appendices
VERMELLES	1·10·15		Ref Map LOOS Sheet 36.C A NW3 1/10,000 PONT A VENDIN 36.3 44	W.Wallis
	2.10.15		In reserve. Batt training & recreation	W.Wallis
	3.10.15		"	W.Wallis
	4·10·15		"	W.Wallis
	5·10·15		"	W.Wallis
	6·10·15		"	W.Wallis
	7·10·15		"	W.Wallis
	8·10·15		"	W.Wallis
	9·10·15		"	W.Wallis
LINE	10·10·15		Th. Batt relieved the 13th B. The Royal Rest in Right subsector of Bab front. Bn HQ H.27.a.50.55. A Coy Right Front Coy, Coy HQ at H.29.a.63. C Coy left front Coy, Coy HQ at H.23.c.4.5. B Coy support Coy with HQ at H.27.c.03. D Coy Reserve Coy with HQ at H.27.b.03. Bn HQ at H.27.a.50.56	W.Wallis
LINE	11·10·15		LINE very quiet	W.Wallis

WAR DIARY

9th Battn (Hrs) The Royal Scots

OCTOBER 1918

WAR DIARY
or
INTELLIGENCE SUMMARY.

(Erase heading not required.)

Army Form C. 2118.

Place	Date	Hour	Summary of Events and Information	Remarks and references to Appendices
VENDIN LE VIEIL	12.10.18	16.30	Ref Map 44A N.W. Edition 11A Laos m:44A 1/10,000. A & C Companies attacked and captured enemy system of posts in VENDIN LE VIEIL. West side of HAUTE DEULE CANAL. Operation entirely successful. 2 Light & 2 heavy machine guns and 35 prisoners captured.	Wilts
do	13.10.18		Consolidating and establishing posts on CANAL BANK	Wilts
do	14.10.18		do	Wilts
do	15.10.18	9.00	Enemy seen to be retiring. A & C Coy crossed HAUTE DEULE CANAL, advanced and took up a line running SOUTH from FOSSE 6. B & C Coys moved forward and occupied positions vacated by A & C Coy in VENDIN LE VIEIL. Battn. H.Q. moved forward to H.24.b.6.6. in VENDIN LE VIEIL.	Wilts
EPINOY & CARVIN	16.10.18		A & C Coy continued to advance and entered villages of EPINOY and CARVIN. Battn. H.Q. moved forward to QUARRY in PONT.A.VENDIN at I.19.c.9.2. In afternoon A & C Coys advanced and made good BOIS D'EPINOY. B Coy H.Q. moved forward to FOSSE 4 at I.17.a. central	Wilts
ESTEVILLE	17.10.18	06.00	1/8" A.I.S.H. passed through the Battn. then moved forward to billets in ESTEVILLE. Bn. H.Q. Ref Map Nord d'Avesnes in house at I.21.c.17.	Wilts
WAHAGNIES	18.10.18	07.00	Battn. moved by road to WAHAGNIES and were accommodated in billets there. Bn. H.Q. beside CHURCH at J.18.b.9.0.	Wilts

WAR DIARY
or
INTELLIGENCE SUMMARY.

(Erase heading not required.)

Army Form C. 2118.

Place	Date	Hour	Summary of Events and Information	Remarks and references to Appendices
			Ref. Map Sheet A.M.P. 1/100,000 A.M. 1/40,000	
THOURS	19.10.18	07.30	7th Battn. moved by road from WAHAGNIES to THOURS and was accommodated in billets.	Weather
			Battn. H.Q. in CHATEAU DU BRON at I.S.G.64.	
MOUCHIN	20.10.18	07.30	Moved by road to OUVIGNIES where Battn. halted for 3 hours, thence to BOIS DE BERCU halting there for 2 hours	Weather
			thence to MOUCHIN where Battn. went into billets.	
BASSE RUE	21.10.18	11.00	7th Battn. moved by road, B & C Coys to BAS PREAU, D Coy to CLERMAY, A Coy to MIN. de CLERMAY, BN. HQ	Weather
			to CHATEAU DE FLINES at B.24.a. Battn. halted for 2 hours and then moved A & D Coy to BOUDERETS, C Coy	
			to BASSE RUE, B Coy to house in C.11.a.9. Bn. HQ in House c.15.a.7b.	
do	22.10.18		Battn. remained in billets.	Weather
do	23.10.18		A & D Coy moved owing to heavy shelling of BOUDERETS. A Coy to PETIT RUMES, D Coy to CLERMAY	Weather
do	23-24.10.18		In billets resting and training	Weather
LINE	27.10.18		Relieved 7/5" K.O.S.B. in the line. B Coy Right Front Coy with HQ in HOLLAIN, D Coy Left Front Coy with HQ in	Weather
			TOLLAIN MERLIN. A Coy Right support Coy with HQ in PARADIS, C Coy Left Support Coy in WEZ-VELVAIN. B.H. HQ.	
			in CHATEAU WEZ VELVAIN at C.5.c.0.8. Line very quiet. Some gas shelling at night.	
LINE	25.10.18		Very quiet during day. Weather bright.	Weather
LINE	29.10.19	00.15 05.00	Bn. HQ & VILLAGE heavily shelled with gas shells 2 & 3000 shells being used.	Weather
	29.10.18	17.00	Relieved by 4/5" B. Black Watch and arrived back to billets in DEROOERIE & CLERMAY.	Weather

WAR DIARY
or
~~INTELLIGENCE~~ SUMMARY.

(Erase heading not required.)

Army Form C. 2118.

Place	Date	Hour	Summary of Events and Information	Remarks and references to Appendices
DERADERIE	2.10.18 to 31.10.18	Ref Map Sheet 44. 1/40,000	In billets clearing up and training.	Weather
			Reinforcement for the month 2/L A.D. GRAY, 2/L A.F. EDGAR, A.H SHIRLAW, A.W.M. MORRIS, 2/L A.H. PORTEOUS and 85 O.R.	
			Casualties for the month Killed 2/L A.A. FORSYTH 3. 6 OR. Wounded 77 OR. missing 3 OR.	Windy

A Stevenson
Lieut Colonel
Comdg 9th B. (Rif) The Royal Scots

SECRET   OPERATION ORDER NO. 30   Copy No. 11

Reference Maps:-
   44a N.W. 1/20,000
                                                    9th October 1918.

1. The 1/9th Bn. (Highlanders) The Royal Scots will relieve the 13th Bn. The Royal Scots in the Right Sub-sector of the Brigade Front tomorrow afternoon.

2. One Officer and one N.C.O. per Company and one N.C.O. for Bn. H.Q. will report at H.Q. 13th Bn. R. Scots at 10.00 for the purpose of taking over Trench Stores, Programme of Work and Defence Schemes etc. Lists will be forwarded to Bn. H.Q. by 10.00 on the 11th.

3. The Battalion will move by Platoons at ten minute intervals. The order of march will be "C" "A" "B" Coys Bn. H.Q. and "D" Coy. The first Platoon of "C" Coy will move at 12.30 hours. Platoons will halt independently at ten minutes to each hour, irrespective of distance travelled, so that correct intervals may be retained.

4. Route will be as follows:- BREWERY VERMELLES, CHURCH VERMELLES thence through G.14.a and c and 20.a to junction of Railway and BETHUNE ROAD, thence by BETHUNE ROAD to point where guides are met.

5. Guides four per Company and two for Bn. H.Q. will be met at point G.34.d.8.4.

6. Lewis Guns and Mess kits will be loaded at 12.00. Limbers will be in Square of Brewery at that hour. One N.C.O. per Company will be detailed to accompany limbers to a point about G.31.a.5.3. where Guns and Mess Kit will be unloaded. This N.C.O. will remain until Coys have removed their Guns and Mess Kit.

7. Waterbottles will be filled before Coys move off. Further water will be sent up in petrol tins with rations at night. These petrol tins must be brought out when Bn. is relieved.

8. Rations for 11th inst., will be carried to the two forward Coys by "D" Coy. O.C. "D" Coy will detail parties for this purpose to be at junction of HUMBUG TRENCH and HARRY ROAD H.27.b.7.1. at 20.00 hours. "B" Coy will carry their own rations and O.C. "B" Coy will detail a party for this purpose to be at above place at the same hour. Rations for "D" Coy and Bn. H.Q. will be dumped at point H.27.d.5.7. on HARRY ROAD.

9. Greatcoats will be taken into the line.

10. Position of Coys in the line will be:-
    Right Front Coy....... "A" Coy   Coy H.Q. H.29.a. 6.3.
    Left   "   " ......"C" "   "   "   H.23.c. 4.5.
    Support Coy.......... "B" Coy   "   "   M.27.b. 0.3.
    Reserve Coy.......... "D" "   "   "   H.27.b. 0.3.
    Battalion Headquarters H.27.b.0.3. H.27.a.5a.55
    Regimental Aid Post   H.27.d.17.8.

11. Completion of Relief will be wired to Bn. H.Q. using the No. 600.

12. ACKNOWLEDGE.

   Issued at 21.00 hours   Capt. A/Adjt.,
                        1/9th Bn. (Highlanders) The Royal Scots

   DISTRIBUTION
      Copy No. 1 to O.C. A Coy   Copy No. 7 O.C. 13th R.Scots
       "   " 2 " O.C. B "   "   " 8 Adjutant
       "   " 3 " O.C. C "   "   " 9 M.O.
       "   " 4 " O.C. D "   "   " 10 File
       "   " 5 " Q.M.   "   " 11 War Diary
       "   " 6 " T.O.

SECRET   OPERATION ORDER No. 31.

Copy No. ___

Ref. Maps.
    44a N.W. Edition 11a.   9th October 1918.

1. After dusk 10:10:18, the Battalion will extend its frontage and will occupy the front line from the present right boundary to the point where HARVEST TRENCH crosses the road at H.22.b.6.6.

2. The Boundary Point between "A" and C Companies will be at H.23.c.50.35.

3. B and "D" Coys will not move their positions.

4. C Coy will make all necessary arrangements with the unit on its left and will carry out the move as soon as it is dark enough to prevent movement being seen by the enemy.

5. "A" Coy will make the necessary side slip as C Coy moves.

6. All arrangements to be made between O.C. Coys concerned.

7. Report completion to Bn. H.Q. by Code word "VENDIN"

8. ACKNOWLEDGE.

Issued at..... hours.   Capt. & A/Adjt.,
                             1/9th Bn. (Highlanders) The Royal Scots.

War Diary

SECRET. OPERATION ORDER No. 32. Copy No.

Reference Trench Map.
    44a N.W. Edition 11a   9th October 1918.
    and Special Map attached.

INTENTION   1.   The 1/9th Bn. R. Scots in conjunction with the Division on the right, and the 10th Bn. Scottish Rifles on the left will attack the enemy system on the West of the HAUTE DEULE CANAL.

OBJECTIVE   2.   The objectives will be as shown on the attached Special Map. Six Outpost positions will be established at approximately the points shown by red crosses on Map.

ENEMY
DISPOSITIONS   3.   It is not definitely known how the enemy holds the area to be attacked, but it is thought that it is held by small Outposts in the village of VENDIN LE VIEIL. There is a certain number of old Gun pits in the village which probably will have dugouts connected with them or in the vicinity

FORMING UP
FOR ATTACK   4.   At Zero minus one hour the Battalion (less one Coy) will be formed up approximately 200 yards in front of HARVEST TRENCH facing North East.

POSITION OF
COMPANIES.   5.   "A" Company will be in front in sections in file, extended along the "Jumping Off" positions.
"B" Company will be on the right in sections in file and extended from approximately H.29.b.2.4. to H.23.c.9.4. They will lie out about 20 yards in rear of "A" Company.
"C" Coy will be on the left in sections in file and extended from "B" Coys left to H.23.a.2.2. They will be out about 20 yards in rear of "A" Company.
"D" Company will hold HARVEST TRENCH.

DUTIES OF
COMPANIES   6.   "A" Company will move off at Zero hour and pass through the village by the best possible routes to the objectives, where they will at once take up the most suitable fire positions. Two Platoons will occupy the three southern Posts and two Platoons the three northern Posts.
"B" and "C" Companies will move off immediately behind "A" Company, and on reaching the buildings will immediately mop up any dugouts, shelters or buildings. This must be done with the utmost care and the whole place must be systematically searched.
Lewis Guns will accompany "B" and "C" Companies and will engage any possible targets on the flanks or elsewhere.
On completion of the "Mopping Up" "B" and "C" Companies will take up a position in rear of "A" Coys Posts and form a Support Line until further orders are issued.

PRISONERS   7.   All prisoners will be sent back to "D" Company at HARVEST TRENCH and the escort will, after handing them over to "D" Company, return to its own Company. "D" Company will escort prisoners to ....

Page 2.

SPECIAL STORES etc.	8.	A supply of "P" Bombs will be issued for clearing dugouts. Lewis Gun teams will carry .... magazines with each gun. Rifle Grenadiers will each carry two No. 36 bombs and riflemen will each carry two bombs. Each man will carry two sandbags. Waterbottles to be filled before moving to assembly positions. Iron rations to be carried. Battle Order to be worn. Greatcoats to be bundled under Company arrangements and left in a dugout under a guard of two suitable men. Coy signallers to be prepared to carry out visual signalling to a point to be notified later.
FLANKS	9.	**Flanks** Touch with Flanks must be maintained on arrival at the objectives and, if possible, during the advance. Liaison posts with the Scottish Rifles will be established on the left flank at the points marked with a circle.
ARTILLERY AND M.Gs.	10.	The bombardment will open at Zero minus 12 minutes by the projection of harmless gas. At Zero minus 10 minutes the Artillery and Machine Guns will open intense fire on the village of VENDIN and strong points. At Zero hour the Artillery will lift to the western bank of the CANAL. At Zero plus 5 minutes the fire will lift to the eastern bank of the CANAL and points on the East of the CANAL. At Zero Livens projectors will fire smoke shell on to the eastern bank of the CANAL.
STOKES MORTARS	11.	The two Stokes Mortars will advance in the centre of "A" Company and will engage any possible targets.
LEWIS GUNS.	12.	It must be impressed on Lewis Gunners that they must open fire on hostile Machine Guns and any other available targets.
STRETCHER BEARERS	13.	Stretcher Bearers will move forward with their Coys.
R.A.P.	14.	Regimental Aid Post will be at................
Battalion H.Q.	15.	Battalion Headquarters will be at................
Machine GUNS	16.	Four Machine Guns will be attached to the Battalion. These will move forward with "A" Coy and take up suitable positions on arrival at the objective
REPORTS.	17.	Reports to be sent to Bn. H.Q. as frequently as possible. Estimated casualties must be stated. All possible information to be forwarded. Negative information may be as useful as positive.
COMMAND	18.	In the event of casualties the command of a unit will pass automatically to the next senior.
INITIATIVE	19.	In an operation of this nature each section or group must necessarily act largely on its own initiative and the main point to keep in view is that a forward movement must be maintained. The "Moppers Up" are likely to reach the objectives some considerable time after the first assaulting line, but it must be remembered that it is actually present as a supporting force

Page 3.

ZERO 20. Zero day is ....

Zero hour is ....

PAPERS etc. 21. No Maps, Papers, sketches etc., likely to be of use to the enemy if captured, except those connected with this operation, are to be taken into action.

These orders are not to be taken beyond Coy H.Q. under any circumstances.

22. ACKNOWLEDGE.

[signature]
Capt. & A/Adjt.,
1/9th Bn. (Highlanders) The Royal Scots

DISTRIBUTION

Copy No. 1 to O.C. A Coy   Copy No. 7 to File
  "   " 2 " O.C. B Coy   "   " 8 " War Diary
  "   " 3 " O.C. C Coy   "   " 9 " Bn. Rt. Flank
  "   " 4 " O.C. D Coy   "   " 10 " Bn. Lt. Flank
  "   " 5 " M.O.   "   " 11 " Brigade
  "   " 6 " Adjutant   "   " 12 " Sig. Officer
                               "   " 13 " 2Lt R. Marshall

SECRET   OPERATION ORDER No. 32
                                 PART II

Ref. French Map
     44a N.W. Edition 11a   10th October 1918.
     and Special Map.

1. The following amendments and additions will be made to Operation
   Order No. 32 issued 9th October 1918.

2. One Company of K.O.S.B. will occupy the outposts along the
   Battalion front at dusk on 11th inst. "B" and "C" Coys will
   then withdraw their Outposts and the Sections relieved will
   rejoin their Companys.

3. The K.O.S.B. in the Outpost line will not move at Zero, and after
   the assaulting troops have passed through their posts, they will
   remain in position.

4. "A" Company will occupy the four northerly Posts on the Battalion
   frontage and "D" Company will detail one platoon to assault and
   occupy the southerly Posts.

5. "A" Company will form a Liaison Post on its left with the Scottish
   Rifles.

6. A tape will be laid out along the line H.23.c.5.5. to H.29.b.5.1.
   This will be laid by Bn. H.Q. and is to serve as a guide for
   forming up.

7. Battle Bn. H.Q. and Advanced R.A.P. will be at the present Coy H.Q.
   at H.23.c.3.6.

8. The Barrage has been altered and will now be as follows:-
   (a) Zero to Zero plus ten - On eastern half of VENDIN and Strong
                                points.
   (b) Zero plus 10 to Zero plus 20 - On eastern side of VENDIN
   (c) Zero plus 20 to Zero plus 23 - On railway lines.
   (d) Zero plus 23 to Zero plus 26 - On west bank of CANAL and
                                       Strong points.
   (e) Zero plus 26   - Lifts to protective Barrage Line.
   Projectors will be fired at Zero minus 2.

9. The assaulting troops will move as follows:-
      Zero plus 5 .... Move forward as close as possible
      (i.e. 7 minutes after   under Barrage (which will be 18 pdr.)
       projectors are fired)
      Zero plus 10 .... Move through village. Barrage will
                                    be only on extreme eastern side.
      Zero plus 26 .... Whole of country west of CANAL free
                                    of Barrage, and whole village clear
                                    of shelling.
   Owing to the distance to be covered it should be impossible for the
   Assaulting Troops to run into the Barrage. The lines of Barrage will
   be clearly visible and in definite lines after Zero plus 10 when the
   destructive shoot on the village is completed.

10. Two platoons of Scottish Rifles will be held in our lines in readiness
    to proceed to the right flank of their own Battalion. These will not
    be available for any other purpose.

11. The unexpired portion of the day's ration will be carried on the men.

12. Hot tea will if possible be provided under Coy. arrangements before
    men move off to jumping off positions.

13. The K.O.S.B. in the Outpost line will ring German Gas Gongs when the
    Projectors are fired at Zero minus 2 minutes. Our troops must be
    warned of this ruse which is being carried out with a view to making
    the enemy put on his Gas Helmet.

14. ACKNOWLEDGE.
                                            Capt. & A/Adjt.,
       DISTRIBUTION   1/9th Bn. (Highlanders) The Royal Scots
       To all recipients of Operation Order No. 32.

SECRET   Appx N° 7

OPERATION ORDERS N° 3?

Ref Map FRANCE 1:40,000 N/40000

The Battn will move by march route today, in ref to THOUARS (K 21 0 6)

Starting Time 08.40 hours

Starting Point EAST end of village (K 18 o.6.9.)

Order of March Bn HQ A-B-C-D Coys and
          Echelon A Transport

ROUTE DEUX VILLES - LOEFRANTIE -
MARTINVAL - LA VERDERIE - MOLPAS -
THOUARS

Echelon A Transport move with the
Battalion. Echelon B in rear of Bde
column.

The Battn will pass Brigade
Starting Point K21 6.13 at
09.30 hrs

2.

Echelon B will pass Bde Starting
Point at 10:10 hours.

Billeting party will meet Staff Captain
at Cross Roads E.10.b.0.3 at 09.00h.

Cop. 1 : 1 b o c 1 bo   Sgd J. Back 2/Lt
      2   " B   Adjy 7 DLI
      3   " C
      4   " D   04.15h.
      5   Tn   19-10-18
      6   QM
      7   WAR DIARY

SECRET Copy n° 1

O O N° 34

Ref maps
   Sheet n° 37 d 44 1/40000

1. The Battn will relieve the 7/8th KOSB on the Bde front, tomorrow 27.10.18 as follows
   A Coy 9th Royal Scot relieves Right Support Coy KOSB
   B "   do   " Right Front Coy
   C "   do   " Left Support Coy
   D "   do   " Left Front Coy

2. Guides will be met at the road junction C.10.c.75.75. This point is to be passed at the following times:—
   A Coy   14.45 hours
   B "   14.15   "
   C "   13.15   "
   D "   13.45   "
   Movement will be by platoons at 200 yd intervals.

3. Cooking arrangements will be the same as those carried out by the KOSB.

4. The greatest care will be exercised in taking over all details of posts, picquets, patrols etc from the outgoing unit

2.

5. Battn Hqrs will be at the chateau WEZ VELVAIN

6. Acknowledge

R.Marshall
2/Lt a/adjt

25.10.18   DU QE

DISTRIBUTION
Copy No 1   O.C A Coy
     2   " B "
     3   " C "
     4   " D "
     5   " 7/8 KOSB
     6   OM & TO
     7   War Diary
     8   File

Addition
7. Completion of relief to be reported to
Bn HQ by use of code word "APPLE"

Copy. OPERATION ORDER.

Ref Map 44ᵈ NW of Ypres

1. The new Battn frontage will be on a line drawn from DISTILLERY in I.7.a. Northeastwards to I.15.b.12 (approx)

2. The line will be held by D Coy and B Coy in front and A & C Coys in Reserve.

3. Boundaries will be as follows:—
D Coy from DISTILLERY to approx I.21.a.8.4. and B Coy from that point to approx I.15.b.12.

  A Coy on relief will move into positions in I.20.b & d.
  C Coy on relief will move into positions between Railway in I.19.b. and I.13.b.87

4. The move will take place immediately on receipt of these orders

5. Companies will report completion of move and give position of post occupied and Company Hqrs.

6. Orders regarding rations will be sent later.

7. Acknowledge.

(Sgd) Harterton
Capt & Adjt

1540 hours
15.10.18   DOOE

Confidential

VOLUME 46

War Diary

9th Battn: (H.S.) The Royal Scots.

From - 1.11.18.
To - 30.11.18.

Army Form C. 2118.

WAR DIARY
or
INTELLIGENCE SUMMARY.
(Erase heading not required.)

Instructions regarding War Diaries and Intelligence Summaries are contained in F.S. Regs., Part II. and the Staff Manual respectively. Title pages will be prepared in manuscript.

Place	Date	Hour	Summary of Events and Information	Remarks and references to Appendices
Ref Maps	Ref 1:40,000 " 1:87	1:40,000 1:40,000		
DERODERIE	1 & 7 Nov 1918		The Battalion remained in billets, training in attack and defence being carried out under Bn arrangements	
do	8-11-18	-	Enemy reported to be retiring. Batt. under short notice to move forward	
BASSE RUE JOLLAIN MERLIN HOLLAIN	9-11-18	08-20 13-00	The Bn moved to BASSE RUE. Batt. HQ remaining in DERODERIE. Received orders for further move to JOLLAIN MERLIN & HOLLAIN. Batt. moved by march route at 1300 hrs. B. Ho A & D Coys in JOLLAIN MERLIN, B & C Coys in HOLLAIN	
PIPAIX	10-11-18	-	The Batt moved by march route to PIPAIX and was billeted there overnight	
Ref Map TOURNAI no 5		1:40,000 Ref 45 1:40,000 Ref 35 1:20,000		
ERVAUX BLICQUY ORMEIGNIES	11-11-18		The Batt. was ordered to proceed to ERVAUX by march route but on arrival there was ordered to push forward to SOUTHERN outskirts of BLICQUY when it was officially announced that an Armistice had been signed and had come into operation. The Batt. then moved to ORMEIGNIES arriving at 1600 hours. A halt for 2 hours was made in a field on SOUTHERN outskirts of BLICQUY	
ORMEIGNIES	12, 13, 14, 15-11-18	-	Remained in billets. Time devoted to cleaning up and recreational training	
TONGRES NOTRE DAME	16-11-18		Batt. moved to TONGRES NOTRE DAME by march route.	
do	17-22-11-18		In billets. Training in ceremonial drill and cleaning up of equipment by C.o.C Division.	
do	23-11-18		Inspection by G.O.C Division. Classes in English and Arithmetic were started this day	
ATTRE MEVERGNIES	24-11-18	14.30	Batt. moved to ATTRE area by march route. C & D Coys billeted in ATTRE and A & B Coys in MEVERGNIES	
			Batt. Headquarters in CHATEAU ATTRE	

Army Form C. 2118.

WAR DIARY
or
INTELLIGENCE SUMMARY.
(Erase heading not required.)

Instructions regarding War Diaries and Intelligence Summaries are contained in F. S. Regs., Part II. and the Staff Manual respectively. Title pages will be prepared in manuscript.

Place	Date	Hour	Summary of Events and Information	Remarks and references to Appendices
ATTRE MEVERGNIES	25.6.24.15	—	L. Bells. Brigade Sports held at BRUGELETTE	Weather
do	27.6.1115	—	L Bells Training in ceremonial drill carried out also recreational training under Coy arrangements	
			Casualties Nil	
			Reinforcements 2/Lieut S.D.M. 46 S.t 15 and 132 O.R.	

McPherson
Lieut Colonel
Cmdg 9th B. (Rd) The Royal Scots

SECRET.   OPERATION ORDER NO 36.   Copy No. 9

REFERENCE MAPS.
Sheet 44.1/40,000

1. **MOVE.** The Battalion will move tomorrow to BASSE RUE, taking over the billets at present occupied by DOLU.

2. **STARTING TIME & STARTING PLACE.** Companies will parade at 08.30 Hours and march independently to new billets.

3. **DRESS.** Marching Order. Greatcoats will be carried.

4. **BILLETS.** Exact locations of Company billets will be notified later.

5. **BILLETING PARTY.** A Billeting Party consisting of 2/Lieut. H.PATERSON and one N.C.O. per platoon will proceed to BASSE RUE at 07.30 to take over billets. "A" Company will find accommodation for the Trench Mortar Team.

6. **LEWIS GUNS & COOKERS.** Lewis Gun limbers and Cookers will accompany their Companies.

7. **VALISES AND BLANKETS.** Blankets will be rolled in bundles of ten and stacked at Quartermaster Stores by 07.30 Hours.

    Officers valises will be collected from Company H.Q. and Battalion H.Q. commencing with "C" Company 08.00 hours. Officers servants will accompany the wagon.

8. **MESS STORES.** Officers Mess Cart will collect box from each Company and Battalion H.Q. commencing with "C" Company at 08.00 Hours.

ACKNOWLEDGE.

8th. November, 1918.

                                                    W M Morris
                                                    Lieut. & A/Adjt.
                                                    9th. Royal Scots.

Copy No.1. to O.C. A Coy   Copy No. 7. 2/Lieut.H.PATERSON
 "   " 2 " O.C. B "   "   "   8. M.O.
 "   " 3 " O.C. C "   "   "   9. War Diary
 "   " 4 " O.C. D "   "   " 10. Adjutant
 "   " 5 " Q.M.   "   " 11. File
 "   " 6 " T.O.

OPERATION ORDER NO.34 (CONTINUED)

9. **BILLETS.** The various billets are adjacent to the following points:-

Battalion H.Q.	"	C.13.a.2.7.
A Company	"	C.7.a.3.0.
B "	"	C.8.d.0.1.
C "	"	C.13.a.2.7.
D "	"	C.7.d.9.0.
Aid Post	"	C.8.d.0.1.
Transport &) Quartermaster Stores)		C.3.c.7.5.

10. **TRANSPORT.** The Transport Officer will arrange to move the Transport to their new situation by 10.00 Hours.

11. **QUARTERMASTER STORES.** The Quartermaster will arrange with the Transport Officer to have all stores moved to new situation by 10.00 Hours.

12. **ROUTES.** The Transport Officer will ensure that all Transport follows the routes laid down by XV Divisional Orders.

13. **MARCHING PARTY.** N.C.Os of each Company detailed in para.8. will proceed by shortest route to new billets.

2/Lieut. H. PATERSON will supervise the whole.

14. **MEDICAL STORES.** The Maltease Cart will collect the Medical Stores at the Regimental Aid Post at 08.30 Hours.

W A Moore
Lieut. & A/Adjt.
9th. Royal Scots.

8th. November, 1918.

ACKNOWLEDGE:-

To all recipients of Operation Order No.34.

SECRET.   OPERATION ORDER NO.37.   Copy No....10....

Reference Maps.
Sheet 44.1/40,000

1. **MOVE.** The Battalion will move today to JOLLAIN MERLIN and
              HOLLAIN at 13.00 Hours.

2. **ROUTES.** Companies will proceed by GUIGNIES - C.4.a. and
              b - WEZ-VELVAIN - C.12.a.

3. **ORDER OF MARCH.** B,C,D,A Companies. Battalion H.Q.
              Transport will move independently by above route.
              200 Yards distance to be maintained between
              Companies.

4. **STARTING POINT.** Leading Company will pass Starting
              point at Road Junction C.3.b.3.2. at 13.45 Hours.

5. **LEWIS GUN AND**   Will move with Companies.
   COOKERS.

6. **SURPLUS KIT AND** If surplus kit, haversacks, mess boxes &c.
   MESS BOXES.   have not been collected they will be
              left at present billets under small guard, which
              will rejoin Companies after kit has been collected.

ACKNOWLEDGE.

                                        W M Morr[y]
9th.November,1918.
                                        Lieut. & A/Adjt.
                                        9th. Royal Scots.

Copy No.1. to O.C. A Coy   Copy No.7 to Commanding Officer
  "   "2 " O.C. B "   "   " 8 " Major W.C.S.LINDSAY
  "   "3 " O.C. C "   "   " 9 " M.O.
  "   "4 " O.C. D "   "   "10 " War Diary
  "   "5 " Q.M.   "   "11 " Adjutant
  "   "6 " T.O.   "   "12 " File.

SECRET   OPERATION ORDER NO.33.   Copy No. 11

Reference Maps.
Sheet 37.1/40,000
Sheet 44.1/40,000

1. MOVE.   The Battalion will move to PIPAIX today, 10th.inst.
            (X.8. a. & b. Sheet 37)

2. ORDER OF MARCH. H.Q., & C.A. & D Companies – Transport –
            200 Yards between Companies.

3. STARTING TIME.   H.Q., A Company and D Company and Transport
            will leave JOLLAIN MERLIN at 05.40 Hours, head
            of column will be at C.12.b.9.4. at 05.35 Hours.
                B & C Companies will parade at HOLLAIN –
            head of B Company to be at road junction
            D.8.a.7.9. (Sheet 44), and proceed with remainder
            of Battalion at approximately 06.10 Hours.

4. BILLETING PARTY. Lieut. J.G. STEEL, mounted, and 1 N.C.O. per
            Company on bicycles, will proceed as Billeting
            Party.   Lieut. STEEL will be responsible for
            Transport and H.Q. Company.   He will leave
            JOLLAIN-MERLIN at 05.40 Hours with N.C.Os of A & D
            Companies and pick up those of B & C Companies, at
            Road Junction D.8.a.7.9. at approximately 05.55
            Hours.

ACKNOWLEDGE.
                                W.M. Morris
10th. November, 1918.
                                Lieut. & A/Adjt.
                                9th. Royal Scots.

Copy No.1. to O.C. A Coy   Copy No.8. to Commanding Officer
  "   " 2 " O.C. B   "   " 9 " Major LINDSAY
  "   " 3 " O.C. C "   "   " 10 " Lieut. J.G. STEEL
  "   " 4 " O.C. D   "   " 11 " War Diary
  "   " 5 " Q.M.   "   " 12 " Adjutant
  "   " 6 " T.O.   "   " 13 " File.
  "   " 7 " M.O.

SECRET   OPERATION ORDER No.39   Copy No. 11

Reference:Maps
Sheets 37 and
TOURNAI 5., 1:40,000.

1. MOVE.   The Battalion will move to ERVEAU today, 11th.inst.
                  (TOURNAI 5.,39.E.5)

2. ORDER OF MARCH. H.Q., A.B.C. & D Companies and Transport. - 200 yards
                     between Companies.

3. STARTING PLACE & The head of the column will move from Point
    TIME   X.E.0.9.7. (Sheet 37) at 08.30 Hours and the
                      remainder will follow at the distance ordered.

4. BILLETING PARTY. 2/Lieut. R.J. KILBURN mounted, and 1 N.C.O. for
                      Q.M.Stores, Transport and 1 N.C.O. per Company, on
                      bicycles, will proceed as Billeting Party, leaving RIPAIX
                      at 06.15 Hours.

5. BAND.   Packs of Pipes and Drums will be stacked for loading at
                  Q.M.Stores by 08.00 Hours.

6. OFFICERS VALISES. Officers valises will be stacked at Q.M.Stores by
                       07.45 Hours for loading.

7. ORDERLY ROOM BOXES. Orderly Room boxes will be at Q.M.Stores
                         ready for loading at 07.45 Hours

8. REGIMENTAL SCOUTS. Sgt WOOD will detail from Battalion Scouts, 1
                        Junior N.C.O. and 2 Privates to proceed at 06.00 Hours by
                        RIPAIX - ST.GENIN - ERVAUX to Reconnoitre roads and
                        direct Battalion.

9. BRIGADE REPORT CENTRE. Major H.O.S. LINDSAY M.C. will report with
                            the mounted orderlies at Brigade Report Centre at Cross
                            Roads half-mile S.E. of A HAUTEUPAN (TOURNAI Sheet 5) at
                            10.00 Hours.

10. MARCH DISCIPLINE. The Commanding Officer considers that the march
                      discipline yesterday was very good and congratulates all
                      ranks in the manner in which it was maintained.

ACKNOWLEDGE.
                                                    W M Morris
11th. November, 1918.
                                                   Lieut. & A/Adjt.
                                                   9th. Royal Scots.

DISTRIBUTION:/-

Copy No.1. to O.C. A Coy
"   " 2. " O.C. B "
"   " 3. " O.C. C "
"   " 4. " O.C. D "
"   " 5. " Q.M.
"   " 6. " T.O.
"   " 7. " M.O.

Copy No.8 to Commanding Officer
"   " 9   Major T.C.S.LINDSAY M.C.
"   " 10" 2/Lieut.R.J.HEPBURN
"   " 11" War Diary
"   " 12" Adjutant
"   " 13" File

SECRET OPERATION ORDER NO.41.   Copy No..12..

Reference Maps.
Sheets 'J' and
TOURNAI 6.

1. **MOVE.** The Battalion will move to ASTER and MEVERGNIES tomorrow 24th.inst.

2. **TIME & PLACE OF PARADE.** Battalion will parade in close column of companies in the Square at TONGRE-NOTRE-DAME at 14.25. Markers at 14.20. Transport will follow from wagon lines when Battalion moves off.

3. **COMPANY LIMBERS AND COOKERS.** Limbers will follow Companies. Cookers will be in rear of Battalion.

4. **BAND.** Packs of pipes and Drums will be stacked for loading at Q.M.Stores by 13.00 hours.

5. **OFFICERS VALISES.** Officers valises will be stacked at Bn & Coy H.Q. for loading by 0830 hours.

6. **ORDERLY ROOM BOXES.** Orderly Room boxes will be at Q.M.Stores for loading by 13.00 hours.

7. **BLANKETS.** One blanket per man will be carried rolled on the top of the pack. The remainder will be rolled in bundles of ten and will be stacked at Q.M.Stores for loading by 0830 hours.

8. **MESS BOXES.** Mess boxes will be ready for lifting at Battalion and Company H.Q. by 13.45 Hours.

9. **BILLETS.** Company Commanders and Transport Officer will render certificates that all billets have been inspected by an Officer after being vacated, and found clean, and that all latrines have been filled up.

ACKNOWLEDGE.

23rd.November,1918.

W M Moore
Capt & A/Adjt.
9th.Royal Scots.

Copy No.1. to O.C. A Coy   Copy No.8 to Commanding Officer
"   "2   " O.C. B "   "   "9   " Major LINDSAY
"   "3   " O.C. C "   "   "10 " War Diary
"   "4   " O.C. D "   "   "11 " Adjutant
"   "5   " Q.M.   "   "12 " File
"   "6   " T.O.
"   "7   " M.O.

WAR DIARY

9th Bn (HRS) The Royal Scots

From 1st Decr 1918
To 31st Decr 1918

VOLUME No 47

(6392) Wt. W6192/P875 1,500,000 4/18 McA & W Ltd (E 2815) Forms W3091/4.   Army Form W.3091.

Cover for Documents.

Nature of Enclosures.

Notes, or Letters written.

Army Form C. 2118.

WAR DIARY
INTELLIGENCE SUMMARY
(Erase heading not required.)

Instructions regarding War Diaries and Intelligence Summaries are contained in F. S. Regs., Part II. and the Staff Manual respectively. Title pages will be prepared in manuscript.

Place	Date	Hour	Summary of Events and Information	Remarks and references to Appendices
ATTRE & MEVERGNIES	1st/4-12-18		In billets. Recreational training carried out.	
DO	5-12-18		Party of 9 Officers and 135 OR including Commanding Officer and Adjutant proceed to WILLAPUIS by march route. Remainder of Battn. carried out educational and recreational training.	
DO	6-12-18		Party at WILLAPUIS proceed to line the road to welcome His Majesty King George on his visit to the Corps Area. Remainder of the Battn. carried out educational and recreational training	
DO	7-12-18		Party returned from WILLAPUIS by march route arriving at ATTRE at 1600 hours. Remainder of the Battn. carried out Educational and recreation training	
DO	8 & 15-12-18		In billets. Educational and recreational training carried out. Demobilisation of miners started 14-12-18	
SOIGNIES	16-12-18		The Battn. moved by march route to SOIGNIES arriving there at 13.30 hours and was billeted there for the night	
TUBIZE	17-12-18		The Battn. moved by march route to TUBIZE arriving there at 13.30 hours and was billeted there for the night	
BRAINE L'ALLEUD	18-12-18		The Battn. moved by march route to BRAINE L'ALLEUD arriving there at 13.30 hours	
DO	19-31-12-18		In Billets. Educational and Recreational training carried out.	
			Casualties Nil	
			Reinforcements. 15 OR. Lieut J.A. McDONALD joined 2-12-18	

Signed
Comdg 9th Bn (Hr) The Royal Scots
Lieut Colonel

SECRET.   OPERATION ORDER NO.42.

Reference Maps:-   Copy No. 12

1. **MOVE.**   The party already detailed will move to WILLAPUIS tomorrow.

2. **STARTING TIME AND PLACE.**   The party will parade at the Orderly Room ready to move at off at 09.30 Hours.

3. **DRESS.**   Officers will wear marching order Sam Browne Belt. Other Ranks with full marching order with haversack, but without steel helmet, or small box respirator. Greatcoats, Waterproof sheets, Mess Tins and necessary cleaning kit must be carried. Surplus kit will be left in safe custody under Company arrangements.

4. **STRENGTH.**   The strength of the party will be 9 Officers and 135 O.R. as follows:-

Headquarters.	2 Officers	32 Other Ranks.
A Company	2 "	26 "
B "	1 "	25 "
C "	2 "	26 "
D "	2 "	25 "
Transport	—	1 "
	9 "	135 "

5. **RATIONS.**   Cooks,(1 from A Coy & 1 from C Coy) as detailed, with B Company Cooker will collect from Companies and Headquarters, the unexpended portion of the rations for 6th.inst, for Other Ranks. Dinner will be cooked en route. Quartermaster will arrange for rations for whole party for 7th.inst. to be taken to WILLAPUIS on 6th.inst.

6. **BLANKETS.**   One per man, rolled in bundles of ten, will be at Orderly Room at 08.45 Hours for loading.

7. **BAND.**   Will wear belts only. Packs will be stacked at Orderly Room at 08.45 Hours for loading.

8. **OFFICERS VALISES.**   Will be at Company Headquarters for loading at 08.15 Hours.

9. **GROOMS.**   Company Commanders riding will not take a groom, but may take a groom batman.

10. **TRANSPORT.**   Will be provided under Brigade Arrangements.

11. **BILLETING OFFICER.**   Captain W.P.STEEL will be prepared to go in advance as Billeting Officer.

ACKNOWLEDGE.

5th.December,1918.

WM Moor
Capt & A/Adjt.
9th.Royal Scots.

Copy No.1. to O.C. A Coy
 "   "   2 " O.C. B "
 "   "   3 " O.C. C "
 "   "   4 " O.C. D "
 "   "   5   Commanding Officer
 "   "   6   Major LINDSAY
 "   "   7   T.O.
 "   "   8   Q.M.

Copy No.9, to Adjutant
 "   " 10 " R.S.M.
 "   " 11 " Drum Major
 "   " 12 " Sergeant Cook
 "   " 13 " War Diary
 "   " 14 " File

SECRET.   Copy No. 12.

Reference Map.
BELGIUM. Sheet 38.
1/40.000   OPERATION ORDER NO.43.

1. **MOVE.**   The Battalion will move towards New Area on 16th. inst.

2. **ORDER OF MARCH.** Headquarters Details, Band, B, C, D, A Companies.,
   Transport.   Intervals of 10 Yards between Companies - 20 Yards
   between Rear Company and Transport and 30 Yards between Units
   will be maintained.

3. **STARTING TIME** The head of the column will be at the Cross Roads Point
   & PLACE.   O.30.b.4.1. and the remainder will assemble WEST of
                     that Point, ready to move off at 08.35 Hours.

4. **BAGGAGE.**   Will be stacked ready for loading at the following times
                     and places:-   *packs*   Time   Place.
                     C & D Coy. Blankets & H.Q.   07.00   Coy.Q.M.Stores. H.Q.
                                                                   at Orderly Room.
                     A & B   "   "   *packs*   07.30   Coy Q.M.Stores.
                     Officers valises   07.15   Coy H.Q. & Orderly Room
                     Mess Boxes   07.30   "   "   "   "
                     ~~Band Packs~~   ~~07.15~~   ~~Orderly Room~~
                     Orderly Room Boxes   07.15   "   "

5. **QUARTERMASTER'S STORES.** The Quartermaster will arrange with Transport
   Officer direct, and both will receive instructions from 46th.
   Infantry Brigade with regard to extra Transport.

6. **COOKERS AND LEWIS GUN LIMBERS.** Will march with Transport.

7. **MEDICAL STORES.** Medical Officer will arrange to have Maltese Cart
   loaded and at Point of assembly before 8.35 Hours.

8. **BILLETS.**   All billets must be left clean and sanitary. Os.C.
   Companies will render to Adjutant at first halt, a Certificate
   that all billets have been inspected by an Officer, and found
   clean, after the men were paraded. * Lieut. R.M. WHYTOCK will
   arrange for this as regards Headquarters Details.
        * If necessary, small rear parties may be left to fill in
   latrines &c.

ACKNOWLEDGE.
                                                           W M Morris
15th. DECEMBER, 1918.
                                                           Capt & Adjt.
                                                           9th. Royal Scots.

Copy No.1. to O.C. A Coy   Copy No.8 to T.O.
  "   " 2 " O.C. B "   "   " 9 " M.O.
  "   " 3 " O.C. C "   "   " 10 " Adjutant
  "   " 4 " O.C. D "   "   " 11 " Drum Major
  "   " 5 " Commanding Officer   "   " 12 " War Diary
  "   " 6 " Major LINDSAY   "   " 13 " Lieut. WHYTOCK
  "   " 7 " Q.M.   "   " 14 " File

War Diary

SECRET. OPERATION ORDER NO.44 Copy No........

Reference Map.
BELGIUM.Sheet 38.
1/40,000

1. **MOVE.** The Battalion will move to ~~CLABECQ~~ TUBIZE tomorrow.

2. **ORDER OF MARCH.** Headquarters Details, Band, D,C,A & B Companies Transport. Intervals of 10 Yards between Companies -, 20 Yards between Rear Company and Transport and 30 Yards between Units will be maintained.

3. **STARTING TIME AND PLACE.** All Companies will fall in at their billets, Band and H.Q. Details at D Company billet. C,A & B Companies will move off in . . order stated at 0855, H.Q.Details, Band & D Company will move out of D Company billet in time to take head of column, being careful not to obstruct other Units marching out. Transport will follow B Company when column passes Transport billets. The ADJUTANT will guide A, B & C Companies.

4. **BAGGAGE.** (a) Blankets and Packs will be stacked for loading at Company Billets and Orderly Room at 0715.
    (b) Officers Valises at Bn. and Company H.Q. at 0745.
    (c) Officers Mess Boxes at Bn. and Company H.Q. at 08.00 Orderly Room boxes at Orderly Room at 0715.
    Companies will each detail a loading party for Company baggage and will leave a L/Corporal and a Private as guard over any surplus.

5. **QUARTERMASTER'S STORES.** The Quartermaster will arrange with Transport Officer direct.

6. **MEDICAL STORES.** Medical Officer will arrange to have Maltese Cart loaded by 08.30.

7. **BILLETS.** All billets must be left clean and sanitary. Os.C. Companies will render to Adjutant at first halt, a Certificate that all billets have been inspected by an Officer, and found clean, after the men were paraded. * Lieut.R.M.WHYTOCK will arrange for this as regards Headquarters Details.
    * If necessary, small rear parties may be left to fill in latrines &c.

8. **REPORTS.** On arrival at destination, Company Commanders, will within an hour, report to Orderly Room, location of Company Headquarters, whether men are all accommodated, and whether all present or otherwise.

ACKNOWLEDGE.
16TH.DECEMBER,1918.

Capt & Adjt.
9th.Royal Scots.

Copy No.1. to O.C. A Coy	Copy No.8. to T.O.
" " 2 " O.C. B "	" " 9 " M.O.
" " 3 " O.C. C "	" " 10 " Lieut.WHYTOCK
" " 4 " O.C. D "	" " 11 " R.S.M.
" " 5 " Commanding Officer	" " 12 " Adjutant
" " 6 " Major LINDSAY	" " 13 " War Diary
" " 7 " Q.M.	" " 14 " File.

S E C R E T.   Copy No......

Reference Map.   OPERATION ORDER NO.45
BRUSSELS 6.,
1/100,000

1. **MOVE.** The Battalion will move to BRAINE L'ALLEUD tomorrow.

2. **ORDER OF MARCH.** Headquarters Details, Band, D,A,C & B Companies - Transport. Intervals of 10 Yards between Companies - 20 Yards between Rear Company and Transport and 30 Yards between Units will be maintained.

3. **STARTING TIME AND PLACE.** Head of Coeum at 0900 at Railway Crossing 100 Yds. West of E of FORGES, East of TUBIZE.

4. **BAGGAGE.** (a) Blankets and Packs will be stacked for loading at Company Billets and Orderly Room at 0715.
   (b) Officers Valises at Bn. and Company H.Q. at 0745.
   (c) Officers Mess boxes at Bn. and Company H.Q. at 0800.
   Orderly Room boxes at Orderly Room at 0715.
   Companies will each detail a Loading Party for Company baggage and will leave a Lance Corporal and a Private as guard over any surplus.

5. **QUARTERMASTER'S STORES.** The Quartermaster will arrange with the Transport Officer direct.

6. **MEDICAL STORES.** Medical Officer will arrange to have Maltese Cart loaded by 0830.

7. **BILLETS.** All billets must be left clean and sanitary. Os.C.Companies will render to Adjutant at first halt, a Certificate that all billets have been inspected by an Officer, and found clean, after the men were paraded.   * Lieut. R.M.WHYTOCK will arrange for this as regards Headquarters Details.
   * If necessary, small rear parties may be left to fill in latrines &c.

8. **REPORTS.** On arrival at destination, Company Commanders will, within an hour, report to Orderly Room, location of Company Headquarters whether men are all accommodated, and whether all present or otherwise.

ACKNOWLEDGE.
17TH.DECEMBER,1918.

                                                        W M Moore
                                                        Capt & Adjt.
                                                        9th.Royal Scots.

N O T I C E.
The Commanding Officer congratulates all ranks on the excellent marching and march discipline, yesterday and today.
    The march past the G.O.C. Division this morning was exceptionally good and reflects great credit upon the men of the Battalion.

D I S T R I B U T I O N.

Copy No.1. to O.C. A Coy	Copy No.8. to T.O.
" " 2 " O.C. B "	" " 9 " M.O.
" " 3 " O.C. C "	" " 10 " Lieut.WHYTOCK
" " 4 " O.C. D "	" " 11 " R.S.M.
" " 5 " Commanding Officer	" " 12 " Adjutant
" " 6 " Major LINDSAY	" " 13 " WAR DIARY
" " 7 " Q.M.	" " 14 " File

9th.Bn.Highrs.The Royal Scots

Individual Decorations in the 15th.Division
June 1918 to the end of the War

C.M.G.	Lieut.Col.A.Stephenson,D.S.O.,M.C.		New Years Lists
M.C.	a/Capt.R.M.Murray	Soissons Aug.	Immediate Awards
	Lieut.W.S.Leslie	Vendin le Vieil Oct.	
	2/Lieut.J.Haig.		New Years Lists
D.C.M.	351055 Sergt.J.Fraser	Soissons Aug.	Immediate Awards
	352379 L/Sergt.J.Hynds M.M.	Vendin le Vieil Oct.	
	51885 Pte.S.G.Salberg	"	
	351176 Pte.A.Haig	Soissons	New Years Lists
	350106 Cpl.A.Squair	Soissons	
	350566 Pte.A.Simpson	Vendin le Vieil	
Bar to M.M.	350314 Sergt.K.M.Baird,M.M.	Soissons Aug.	Immediate Awards
	352321 Pte.W.Dobbin,M.M.	"	
M.M.	352370 L/Cpl.J.Hynds	Soissons Aug.	Immediate Awards
	352247 Pte.M.Cloughterty		
	352207 Pte.D.S.Brown		
	352087 Pte.H.Macdonald		
	350787 Pte.H.Salmon		
	376054 Pte.H.Wilson		
	44189 L/Cpl.G.Pringle		
	44398 Pte.AJ.Campbell		
	51889 Pte.A.J.Boyne		
	51915 Pte.J.S.Smart		

351110 Sergt.C.Haig	Wez Velvain Oct	M.M.	Immediate Awards
352508 Cpl.J.Todd	Vendin le Vieil Oct.		
352461 Sergt.W.Allan	"		
352285 Pte.J.McGregor	"		
202425 Pte.G.Briggs	"		
30229 L/Cpl.W.F.Clarke	"		
350446 C.Q.M.S.G.S.Bruce		M.S.M.	New Years Lists
350520 C.Q.M.S.T.Wilson			
350050 T/S.M.J.Downie			
350335 Pte.L.E.Thomsen			
Lieut.Col.J.B.Muir,D.S.O.	Soissons Aug.	Croix de Cheval Legion of Honour	Immediate Awards
351055 Sergt.J.Fraser,D.C.M.	"	Medaille Militair	
350314 Sergt.K.M.Baird,M.M.			
Lieut.J.S.Thomsen,M.C.		Croix de Guerre (Palms)	
Lieut.A.J.Hughson			
352231 Pte.W.Dobbin,M.M.			
351101 a/Sergt.A.Leckie		Croix de Guerre (Etoile)	
350979 Pte.W.Blythe			
352558 Pte.W.Pennie			
202661 Pte.A.Cope			
42545 Pte.E.J.McWhirter			
Capt.P.J.Blair (While attached to Division or Brigade Staff)		Croix de Guerre	
351312 Sergt.T.Bruce (Recommended, but not known if award received, though I believe I noticed the name in a List published in the Press) JWN.		Chevalier de l'Ordre de Leopold II	

Volume 47.

Confidential
A

War Diary.

9th Battn (R.) The Royal Scots.

S.N.W.

From 1.1.19.

No. 31.1.19.

(6392) Wt. W6192/P875 1,500,000 4/18 McA & W Ltd (E 2815) Forms W3091/4.

Army Form W.3091.

Cover for Documents.

Nature of Enclosures.

Notes, or Letters written.

Army Form C. 2118.

WAR DIARY
or
INTELLIGENCE SUMMARY.
(Erase heading not required.)

Place	Date	Hour	Summary of Events and Information	Remarks and references to Appendices
BRAINE-L'ALLEUD	1-1-19 - 31-1-19		No fatalities in BRAINE L'ALLEUD. Educational and Recreational training carried out.	
Do	27-1-19		Detachment of the Battn. left the ground for preservation of the Colours of the 2/Bn R.O.S. Borderers.	
			Reinforcements 30 O.Rs.	
			Casualties Nil	
			The following Officers and O.Rs. proceeded for demobilization during the month of January 1919. Capt. M.P. THORBURN (8"RS), A/Capt. R.M. MURRAY (3"RS), LIEUT. H. SHIRLAW (4"RS), 2/LT J. WISHART (2"RS), 2/LT W.S. HEPBURN (4"RS), 2/LT H. PATERSON (3"RS), 2/LT J.R. MARSHALL and 221 O.Rs.	Winter

M Munsary Major
Comdg 9th Bn (R) The Royal Scots

(A 9175) Wt. W4358/1361 6m 000 12/17 D.D.&L. Sch 31m Forms/C2118/15

Confidential

Vol 49

War Diary

9th Battn (½) The Royal Scots.

Vol. 49

From 1-2-19.

To 28.2.19.

45-Rl-

(6392) Wt. W6192/P875 1,500,000 4/18 McA & W Ltd (E 2815) Forms W3091/4.   Army Form W.3091.

Cover for Documents.

Nature of Enclosures.

Notes, or Letters written.

Army Form C. 2118.

WAR DIARY
or
INTELLIGENCE SUMMARY.
(Erase heading not required.)

Place	Date	Hour	Summary of Events and Information	Remarks and references to Appendices
BRAINE L'ALLEUD	1.2.19 to 28.2.19		The Battalion was billeted in BRAINE L'ALLEUD for the month of February. Troops carried out training (Drills, Routemarching etc) daily in the forenoons and Recreational training in the afternoon. Of working party under R.E. was supplied daily from 11th to 19th February. Educational classes were held daily in English, French, Arithmetic, Latin, Practical Gardening and Shorthand. Recreation:- During the month two cups were competed for by the Battalion team. First the Benson Cup (Association football) second the 116th Brigade Athletic Cup. For the Benson cup the Battalion team beat H.Q. Bde H.Q. Team by 6 goals to 3 but were in turn beaten by the 1/2nd K.O.S.B. team by 3 goals to 1. In the competition for the Athletic Cup 9th Royal Scots defeated 1/2nd K.O.S.B. by 1 goal to 0 but were defeated in the Final by the 10th Scottish Rifles by 3 goals to 0. In the Tug of War the 9th Scots were beaten both by the 1/6 K.O.S.B's & the 10th S.R. by two pulls to 0 in each case. In the Cross Country Race the 9th R Scots took 2nd place. In addition to the forgoing competitions, Inter-platoon matches and also Cross Country Runs took place. Boxing:- In the Divisional Boxing Competition held on the 6th & 7th the Battalion was	W.D.S.M

Army Form C. 2118.

WAR DIARY
or
INTELLIGENCE SUMMARY.
(Erase heading not required.)

Place	Date	Hour	Summary of Events and Information	Remarks and references to Appendices
			represented in four trials and good wins were recorded by 62281 Pte W. Davidson (Light-Weight) and 302350 Pte J. Driscoll (Feather Weight). In the semi-final Competition held at Lille the entrants were Pte Davidson & Pte Driscoll. Pte Davidson was defeated. Pte Driscoll put up a sensational bout which had to be settled after extra rounds the verdict going against him on points.	MSM
			During the demobilization of many of the best exponents of sport the high standard hitherto maintained by the battalion could not be reached.	
			During the month the following Officers were demobilised:- Capt. H. Love, Lt Col D. H. Lawson, Lt Col J. Drew, Lt J. E. Banks, Lieut J. of Portis, and 2/Lt E. Latham and also 2/Lt Other Ranks.	
			Reinforcements. During the month 15 Other Ranks reported from Hospital.	
			The weather for the month was good	

A. Stephenson Lt Col
Comm'dg 9th (S) The Royal Scots.

Confidential

Volume No:- 50.

War Diary

9th Bn. (Highlanders) The Royal Scots.

From:- March 1st 1919

To:- March 31st 1919

(6392) Wt. W6192/P875 1,500,000 4/18 McA & W Ltd (E 2815) Forms W3091/4.   Army Form W.3091.

Cover for Documents.

Nature of Enclosures.

Notes, or Letters written.

Army Form C. 2118.

WAR DIARY
INTELLIGENCE SUMMARY.
(Erase heading not required.)

Instructions regarding War Diaries and Intelligence Summaries are contained in F. S. Regs., Part II. and the Staff Manual respectively. Title pages will be prepared in manuscript.

Place	Date	Hour	Summary of Events and Information	Remarks and references to Appendices
Avaurs to Lichteud	1-3-19 to 4-3-19.		The Battalion carried out Company training in the forenoons. Educational Classes were also held between the hours of 10.00 and 12.00 daily. Recreational training was carried out in the afternoons.	Nil
	5-3-19		In accordance with 46th Infantry Brigade Orders, the Battalion left Avaurs L'Olleud at 08.45 hours and proceeded by route march to Aubigs where billets were occupied.	Nil
Aubigs	6-3-19 to 31-3-19.		The Battalion was billeted in Aubigs. Men of the Battalion were mainly employed on fatigue duties in the Divisional and Brigade areas during the period. Owing to the number of men being despatched from time to time for demobilization, Educational Classes had to be dispensed with and very little Recreational training was taken part in. The Battalion however was represented in the Competition for the 46th Infantry Brigade Athletic Cup by No 6329.1 Pte D. Munro + 35029 R.Q.M.S. D. Anderson in the 100 yards and 1 mile flat races. The former Pte D. Munro won the 100	Nil

(A8204) D. D. & L., London, E.C. Wt. W1771/M231 750,000 5/17 Sch. 52 Forms/C2118/14

Army Form C. 2118.

WAR DIARY
INTELLIGENCE SUMMARY
(Erase heading not required.)

Instructions regarding War Diaries and Intelligence Summaries are contained in F.S. Regs., Part II. and the Staff Manual respectively. Title pages will be prepared in manuscript.

Place	Date	Hour	Summary of Events and Information	Remarks and references to Appendices
Jubize	6-3-19 to 31-3-19.		The following Officers proceeded to join the 11th Bn. the Royal Scots	AW
			Capt. W. Bennett Clark. }	
			a/Capt. W.L. Steel. M.C. } MARCH 15th 1919.	
			a/Capt. W.J. Geddie. M.C. }	
			Lieut. A. Black }	
			Lieut. W.B. Mickle }	
			2/Lieut. J. Haig }	
			Lieut. A.O. Gray }	
			Lieut. J. Stephenson M.C. } MARCH 16th 1919.	
			Lieut. A.T. Cameron } MARCH 21st 1919.	
			Lieut. Col. A. Stephenson. D.S.O., D.L.O., M.C., proceeded to U.K. for repatriation on March 28th 1919.	
			Capt. J.G. Burns in the temporary absence of Major W.E.L. Lindsay M.C. on leave assumed command of the Battalion.	AW

M. Burns. Captain
Commanding 9th Bn/Att/the Royal Scots.

Volume 51.

Confidential

War Diary

9th Battn. (A) (R.) The Royal Scots.

From 1.4.19. To 30.4.19.

Army Form C. 2118.

WAR DIARY
INTELLIGENCE SUMMARY.
(Erase heading not required.)

Place	Date	Hour	Summary of Events and Information	Remarks and references to Appendices
TUBIZE BELGIUM	April 1st to April 16 1919		The Battalion was billeted in Tubize during the month of April. Little or no training was carried out owing to the fact that the majority of the men remaining on the strength of the unit were required to furnish Guards and Fatigues with other formations. Orders were received from I.G.H.Q. to despatch, as soon as the men were ready, three drafts of returnable personnel to Tubize 287, 332 and 323 drummers of War being called at the first were completed and despatched on 4th April. Strong to 2 Officers and 80 Other Ranks (Officers 2/Lieut H Eagar - 2/Lieut H Wood) The second escort composed of 80 Other Ranks was despatched to the 332 drummers of War being on 20th April (Conducting Officers 2/Lieut H J G Barclay) of proportion of the third containing 2/Lieut H J G Barclay Ranks was despatched to 323 drummers of War being on 25th April under Conducting Officer 2/Lieut H J Madozah. Capt. G.W.C. Mcaid M.C. 10/Alt H.L.I. in charge of 118th Lyttle Trench Mortar Battery was ordered to and taken on the strength of this unit on 28.3.19. on the twenty of the Battery formerly under his command	

Army Form C. 2118.

WAR DIARY
INTELLIGENCE SUMMARY.
(Erase heading not required.)

Place	Date	Hour	Summary of Events and Information	Remarks and references to Appendices
TUBIZE BELGIUM	APR 1st to APR 30th 1919		Officers who quitted during the month were as under. Capt. A.R.C. Mark M.C. to H.E. for dispersal 23.4.19. Capt. J. Anderson posted to 4th Bn Royal Scots Fusiliers 1-4-19. 2/Lieut A.J.E. Barclay posted to 5th Bn K.O.S.B. 26-4-19. The weather for the month of April was cold and showery. The health of the Battalion was good	

M.W. Humphrey Major
Cmdg 9th Bn/A&SH Royal Scots.

Confidential
Vol 52

48 R

Volume 52

War Diary
9th Batt (the) The Royal Scots.

From:- 1.5.19.
To:- 31.5.19.

Army Form C. 2118.

WAR DIARY
of
INTELLIGENCE SUMMARY. 9⁷ᵗʰ (H.L.I) The Royal Scots

(Erase heading not required.)

Instructions regarding War Diaries and Intelligence Summaries are contained in F. S. Regs., Part II. and the Staff Manual respectively. Title pages will be prepared in manuscript.

Place	Date	Hour	Summary of Events and Information	Remarks and references to Appendices
TURIZE	1-5-19 to 31-5-19		Battalion was billeted in TURIZE during the month of May. No training was carried out the Battalion being practically to Cadre Strength. On 30.5.19 28 or's were despatched from the Unit to complete the Escort of 80 or's ordered for the 323 Prisoners of War Company. Capt. J. S. BURNS proceeded on 21.5.19 to U.K. for demobilization. Sport:- On 28ᵗʰ May the Battalion engaged in a cricket match with the XV Div M.T.Coy.R.A.S.C., and an enjoyable game resulted in a win for the Battalion by 43 runs. The weather for the month was very dry and warm.	

A.W. Lindsay Major
Comm'g 9/3 (H⁴ᵗ) The Royal Scots

www.ingramcontent.com/pod-product-compliance
Lightning Source LLC
Chambersburg PA
CBHW081549160426
43191CB00011B/1873